Making Every Day Count

•

Daily reflections on living as a child of God

by
John Ryeland

ISBN No. 978-1-907636-77-6

Published for John Ryeland by Verité CM Ltd
Worthing, West Sussex UK BN12 4HJ
+44 (0) 1903 241975

Printed in England

Foreword

The Bible – God's written word to us – refers to itself as being like food (Hebrews 5.12; 1 Peter 2.2). And just as there are various ways of making food for us to eat, there are various ways of preparing God's word for our use. The most familiar to us today is what we might call the *methodical* study of Scripture. Here we sit down and read through a long passage, perhaps even an entire book of the Bible, trying to understand it and, possibly aided by commentaries, to comprehend what it meant to its readers when it was written, and what it should mean to us today. Alternatively, but equally methodically, we may decide to go through the Bible tracing some of its great themes, for example, salvation, sacrifice or hope. This methodical and thoughtful way of analysing God's word is utterly essential for all Christians and I recommend it to you without reservation. Yet sadly, and all too often, such study can degenerate into bad reading habits. At best, we amass nothing but facts and at worst, we end up simply with the dubious achievement of having speed-read our way through Scripture. In neither case does God's word really take root in our hearts from where it can affect our lives.

There is an additional way of letting God speak to us through his word, which counterbalances these dangers, and this is the *meditative* study of Scripture. This ancient method involves taking a single short passage, often a single verse or a phrase, and, without denying its original meaning, letting it sink slowly and deeply into our minds and hearts. As we digest it and contemplate all that it means, we may well find God speaking through the Spirit to us with a new clarity and power. It is this pattern of scriptural study that you will find in this stimulating book by my friend, John Ryeland.

If you are unfamiliar with this method of studying scripture, you may, by glancing at such short passages and their comments, come to two wrong conclusions. The first is to dismiss these passages as being too brief to be useful. Yet the truth is that sometimes less is more; an arrow may penetrate where a spear cannot. The second danger is to assume that these readings are a time-saving shortcut to allow the busy to read God's word. The truth is otherwise. These are not microwavable, just-add-water, pre-digested, instant meals of spiritual nourishment to be bolted down in the midst of a multitude of other tasks. In fact, the opposite is true. Although the text and commentary may seem slender, to hear God speak through them may require long minutes of reflective thought. In fact, this method of Scripture reading is not a concession to busyness but an antidote to it.

I'm delighted to recommend this collection of daily readings as an introduction to this meditative way of approaching Scripture. Of the many merits of this collection, three qualities strike me:

It is *reverent*. In these pages God – Father, Son and Holy Spirit – takes centre stage. Some daily readings major on personal anecdotes and illustrations but not these; you will learn nothing here of John's family, friends or football team. His business – as ours should be – is God and him alone.

It is *revealing*. There is wisdom here. Time and time again a fragment of Scripture is held up to the light and in it we see untold riches. In some easily overlooked detail of a text we repeatedly find ourselves directed to great and eternal truths. The large is seen in the little.

Finally, it is *relevant*. It is, in fact, doubly relevant: it is relevant to the heavenly matter of knowing God in Christ; and it is relevant to the earthly matters of how we live and love in a world of busyness.

Historians tell us that one of the significant moments in Christian history was when, in AD386, the man whom history has come to know as St Augustine heard a child cry, "Take and read." Taking those words as a command from God, Augustine picked up the Scriptures, read them and was converted. From that phrase arose a mighty man of God. I can say of this book, as it says of Scripture, "Take and read!"

Revd Canon J.John
www.philotrust.com

Introduction

I have always found immense value in starting my day with a 'quiet time'. The question is: what do you do in it? It can be all too easy to sit down, full of good intentions, and either not know what to do with the time, or end up doing all the talking and not sense that God is replying to you! As you read these daily thoughts, my prayer is that you will discover more and more of God's love for you and his presence with you, and that as a result of this you will realise just what a gift you can be to the people around you and the situations you face each day.

My work is in the area of Christian healing, and what I find time and time again is that when everyone involved is open to the extent of God's love and presence with them, prayer for healing becomes so much more natural. As we stand before God with our hearts open to him, we are like children with our arms open wide before a loving parent.

I hope that these daily thoughts will encourage you to be open to God's transforming touch, and not just for seeking healing. They started out being published online as a 'thought for the day', but it soon became evident that they were being used by God to bring a new awareness of his love to people, which in turn had a real impact on their lives. I want to thank those people who have contacted me with words of encouragement over the years. It was this encouragement that prompted me to gather together some of these daily thoughts in this published format.

Although this book carries my name on the front cover, it would not have happened without the help of a number of wonderful people.

I want to thank J John for agreeing to write the foreword. It has been such a privilege to get to know him over the past few years, and I wish everyone could have access to the deep well of encouragement that naturally springs from him and his wife, Killy.

Thanks are also due to Susannah Steel for her much-needed editing skills. Her commitment to seeing this material published and willingness to help has in itself been such an encouragement.

I also want to thank the wonderful staff at The Christian Healing Mission, who are a constant source of support and inspiration, and in particular special thanks must go to Liz Nicoll for her brilliant design skills.

Finally, my thanks to Gillian, my wife, who first saw the vision for this book and has painstakingly read and re-read every word – and still has the grace to say she continues to be blessed by them!

John Ryeland

> **"**_Father, glorify your name!_**"**
> **John 12.28**

A prayer for a new year

As this New Year begins, these words, which Jesus spoke to his Father, are possibly some of the most appropriate words to have on your lips. At this point so much had happened in Jesus' ministry, and he now faced the brutality of the cross and the glory of the resurrection. His prayer is one of total surrender to his Father and a cry that our knowledge of the Father might be increased through him. It is a prayer that the loving character of God the Father would be seen more and more.

You simply have no idea what this year will bring for you, yet as you begin to step into it your prayer can be the prayer of Jesus: that the Father will glorify his name, and the loving character of God the Father, might be seen more and more both by you and through you.

Whatever your dreams and resolutions for the months ahead, if you are able to say at the end of this year that you know more of the Father's loving heart, and that others know more of it because of you, then it will have been a good year.

Take the words, "Father, glorify your name!" and make them your own prayer. Speak them over your work, your family and over every part of your life.

Living for an audience of one

How would we judge someone who is committed to God? We probably all have our own standards and views about what commitment looks like. We may judge it by someone's behaviour, their pattern of prayer, the amount they give or a host of other considerations. To be honest, we can be pretty quick to judge!

This verse points out the very good news that it is not about what we or other people think, but what God thinks. Other people look at your actions, but only God actually sees your heart and its motives.

A wonderful phrase you may sometimes hear is that we should live for 'an audience of one'. In other words, the judgment and opinion you really should be seeking is from God, who in Jesus Christ loved you and gave himself for you. You do not need to seek to impress others, nor worry whether your good deeds have been noticed or if they may have been misinterpreted; you live for an audience of one.

So it is the gaze of God's loving eyes upon your heart that counts, not the eyes of others. He will not wish that you were someone else as you spend some quiet time with him now, but is looking at you with love and enjoying your company.

> **Lord, Son of David, have mercy on us!**
>
> **Matthew 20.30**

Standing in the waterfall

If you think about mercy, you may picture it as being something like a Roman gladiatorial event, of two men fighting: when one gladiator got the upper hand, he had to look to the Emperor in the stands to determine whether or not he should show mercy to his opponent. This act of mercy depended on whether the Emperor was in a good mood or if it had been a good fight.

Is that what the mercy of God is about? Does it depend on God's mood, or on whether you deserve his mercy?

Perhaps a better picture of mercy is that of a waterfall: it flows, and nothing can stop it flowing. When you ask God to have mercy, it is not that you ask him to do something that is contrary to his nature. Rather, you are reminding yourself of what is freely available and always there, and giving yourself permission to stand beneath that waterfall. Often, it is about giving yourself this permission, because so much of the time it is you who is the barrier to God's mercy by feeling you are excluded.

As you come to God in prayer today, you are already standing before a continuous waterfall of his mercy. Begin to believe that it is for you.

Being united with Jesus

> 66 *If you remain in me and my words remain in you, ask whatever you wish, and it will be given you.* 99
> **John 15.7**

The very idea of asking God for whatever you want and it being done for you is quite something. However, this is not what Jesus is promising in this verse. Instead he is saying that prayer will naturally flow as a consequence of a life lived in union with Jesus.

How can you achieve this, especially as you may well not have been called to a monastic or contemplative life? There are things like jobs and tasks to be done and families to look after.

The key is not to see union with Jesus as something requiring you to turn your back on everything else, but instead union with him becomes the context for the whole of your life. It is about seeking to be with Jesus and setting him at the centre of all you do.

You might like to try spending five or ten minutes each day slowly repeating a word or phrase until you consciously absorb it, and then it will come back to you in the hours ahead. There are many words and phrases you might choose, including:
'Jesus'
'Abba'
'I bear your name, LORD God Almighty'
'I am a temple of the Holy Spirit'.

Find a phrase in the Bible that resonates with you, practise absorbing it and discover the joy of a growing sense of his presence today.

The same Jesus, then and now

'Jesus Christ is the same yesterday and today and forever.'
Hebrews 13.8

This sentence is so simple, so comforting and also so challenging. The Jesus you worship and whose presence you seek is the same Jesus you read about in the Gospels. He has the same heart, the same passions and the same love for you.

This is what is so comforting. In your times of need, when perhaps you can identify with some of the sinners, the unclean and the sick that Jesus touched, he has not changed. His heart is moved by your situations just as it was moved back then. It bothers Jesus when you are in pain or are being badly treated. That is why he came to this world – to show you how much it bothered him. He is the same today as he was then; it still bothers him.

The challenge is this: do you actually believe it? If Jesus in physical form was to walk round by your side today, what difference would it make to what you do? If prayer was about actually sitting with the physical Jesus, what would come out of your lips?

As you turn to Jesus now, begin by letting these words take root in you: 'Jesus, you are the same yesterday, today and tomorrow.' Let the truth of that make a difference to you today.

The wonder of the Father | 1

66 *I have made you known to them and will continue to make you known...* **99**
John 17.26

As you read through the Gospels and look at the ministry of Jesus, ask yourself what it was he was seeking to do. Was it to bring salvation to as many as he could? Was it to bring freedom to those who were held captive? Of course, both these reasons are true, but he did more. In this verse, Jesus reveals something wonderful about what was really driving him in his ministry. He came to reveal the nature of the Father.

The whole of John 17 is a prayer – the final prayer between Jesus and his Father before the events of the Passion. In this final verse of the chapter, Jesus speaks to his Father and says that he has indeed made him known, and will continue to do so. In other words, as the events of the Passion unfolded, and as Jesus exercises his ministry among us today, he is still on that mission to make the Father known.

If ever you think you can pray to Jesus rather than the Father because Jesus seems somehow more approachable, you are missing something very important. Everything Jesus did or said showed something beautiful about the Father; you can come to the Father with the same joy and wonder with which you come to Jesus.

> *...in order that the love you have for me may be in them.*
>
> **John 17.26**

He wants to fill you with his love | 2

Jesus' desire to reveal the Father to us is explored further in John 17.26. What Jesus wants is for us to know and live in the same love relationship that he and the Father enjoy. This is a staggering thought – that the same intense, intimate relationship that Jesus and his Father enjoy can be ours too.

You may think of many reasons why this should not be true for you. Yet what Jesus is saying is that first and foremost this is not about you or what you may have done right or wrong. This is about something that was set in motion before the foundation of the world.

The Father and the Son embrace and each hold out an arm for you to approach and become part of that embrace. The first step towards joining them is to say 'yes'. It is not about what you may or may not deserve, it is about what God wants to happen. Ask the Holy Spirit to help you enter into that embrace, and begin to find the love that has been waiting for you since the day you were born.

It's not about your limping, but about your worship!

> 'By faith Jacob... worshipped as he leaned on the top of his staff.'
>
> **Hebrews 11.21**

This is actually a very powerful verse that takes account of our human weaknesses. Jacob used a staff – a walking stick – because he had a limp resulting from a moment in his life when he wrestled with God. In that time of struggle, God touched his leg and from then on Jacob walked with a limp. So this is a beautiful picture of Jacob worshipping God as he leant upon his stick.

You may often try to hide your weaknesses from other people, as you don't want them to see how you really are, but what you cannot do is hide from God. He knows you through and through, your strengths as well as your weaknesses. Yet what he really values is when you stand before him in worship, just being yourself.

We all have wounds, which come from a variety of sources: some may be self-inflicted, some may come from the hands of others and there are some that you might wonder if they come from God. What really counts is standing before him, with all your wounds, worshipping him and acknowledging that he has called you into being and sent Jesus to demonstrate the extent of his love. It is not your limping that is the most important thing about you, but whether you are a worshipper.

‘*God gives the Spirit without limit*’

John 3.34

All of him in all of me

This is a wonderful verse to call to mind whenever you are in need of God. What it means is that God has given you the fullness of the Holy Spirit – not just a part of him, but all of him. This is actually quite logical: the Holy Spirit is a person so he cannot be divided up any more than you can; when you go into a room, every part of you is there, not just a little bit. So it is with the Holy Spirit, whom God has given us. We have his fullness within us. Our trouble is that we either don't know it or we forget to live in the reality of the gift that God has given us.

Whatever situations you face today, the truth is that the full measure of the Holy Spirit has been given to you and you can call upon him and draw on him for every occasion. He is the Spirit who longs to bring fruit to your life; he is the Spirit who brings gifts to you so that you might be a blessing to others; he is the Spirit who is constantly seeking to bring you back to the wonder of God's love for you.

Take a few moments to repeat these words to yourself and let their impact fill you: "The fullness of the Holy Spirit is dwelling in me."

Giving to God

> *He who is kind to the poor lends to the LORD, and he will reward him for what he has done.*
>
> **Proverbs 19.17**

This striking verse reminds us that when we are kind to a person in need our kindness is actually towards God; what we do for others, we really do for God. If we took this verse more seriously we would probably do a lot more to help others! A legitimate question to ask is: "What can I do?" or "Who is it I am meant to help?"

This verse talks about showing kindness to the poor, those who lack something such as money or food, and it may be an act of kindness in giving to someone in such a situation. However, some people's poverty may be of a different nature. They may lack encouragement, company, affirmation or simply someone to notice them.

Today, look for someone who is in need – perhaps simply someone with a downcast face – and show them kindness. Not only will they be touched, but your action will also touch God.

Called by his name | 1

Isaiah uses three phrases to describe us in this verse. These phrases are God's view of us, how he sees us. What's interesting is that his opinion can be so very different from our own.

The first phrase is that you are 'called by his name'. God is not ashamed, embarrassed or apologetic to have his name stamped upon you; instead he is proud to be associated with you.

Jesus prayed that the love the Father had for him would be in you (John 17.26). If this is the extent of the Father's love for you, no wonder he takes pride and joy in you. He sees you through the same proud and loving eyes with which he sees Jesus.

Of course, this can cause a problem because you think you know what you are really like; you know why God should not love you. However, that is exactly the point of this particular phrase – you are called by his name. It is not your decision to be loved by him, and he doesn't even ask you about it; it is his choice, his decision and his calling, and there is nothing you can do about it.

Learning to accept and rest in the love of God is hard, not because of anything you have to do to find it, but because it means turning your back on your own self-image and accepting his deep love for you. Take a moment to ponder your image of yourself and consider these words: 'I am called by his name.'

All about
his glory | 2

We can think so little of ourselves. However, the truth that the Bible reveals is that we have been called by the Father to share in the same relationship with him that Jesus had. We have been called to be a part of the same mission that gripped Jesus, and we have also been created to reveal the glory of God.

It is quite hard to define the word 'glory'. Most of us think of it in terms of light or beauty. It is probably true to say that to reveal the glory of God is to reveal God for who he really is. That is why we have been created. This might seem like we are being set up to fail – how can we, with all our frailties, reveal God for who he really is? Yet if that is what we are created for, if it is what we were designed for, then it must be wholly possible for us to do that.

As you ponder your immediate plans and all the things you know you will be doing – some decided by you, and some planned by others – say these words slowly to yourself, "I am created for his glory." This is what God wants you to take into the day ahead.

Uniquely crafted by God | 3

> 66 *...everyone who is called by my name, whom I created for my glory, whom I formed and made.* 99
>
> **Isaiah 43.7**

The third great truth that God speaks about through this wonderful verse of Isaiah's is your uniqueness and value to God. He formed and made you. The word 'formed' carries the connotation of something that a potter has made by hand. In other words, God has created each one of us uniquely and wonderfully. Perhaps the word that stands out in this third phrase is 'I'. You may agree with the psalmist that you are 'fearfully and wonderfully made' (Psalm 139.14), but this phrase from Isaiah emphasises something more compelling – it is God who has formed and made you; you are not an accident.

You may wonder whether you have any significance at all. You may often compare yourself to others and wish you were more like them. When that happens, you have probably slipped away from the profound truth that the Lord God has created you uniquely.

Take a moment to let the words 'he formed and made me' run through your mind slowly and deliberately. Begin to delight in the truth of those words, and start to catch the delight of the Creator in what he has made.

The proof of God's love

> 'This is how God showed his love among us: He sent his one and only Son into the world that we might live through him.'
>
> **1 John 4.9**

How do I know that God loves me? This is a real question for many people. We are told of God's love, we read of it and we sing of it in hymns and choruses, but how do we know that it is true and real for us? If we are honest, there are many times when we do not feel that love, and God can seem very distant.

What the Bible comes back to again and again is that the love of God is not primarily about feelings (although it's true that on some occasions we may feel his love), but rather his love is proved by what he has already done by sending Jesus to us.

Why would God send Jesus to this world if not to show his love? It can hardly be to judge us. If God wanted to judge and punish us, he could do that anyway; he certainly did not need to come to earth to do so. Yet Jesus, showing an amazing compassion to those who were in need, came from the Father, and through his death he opened the way back to God for us. That is how we know that God loves us.

The next time you pass an image of a cross, whether it's around someone's neck or on top of a building, try to do more than simply note it. Reflect on it and let it be a reminder of God's profound love for you.

God in the here and now

> **"**Build houses and settle down; plant gardens and eat what they produce.**"**
>
> **Jeremiah 29.5**

At this point in his life, Jeremiah was fighting a lonely battle. His nation was in trouble and under oppression. The leaders and the people were longing for God to step in and do something miraculous, and they wanted to listen to anyone who would tell them that this was God's plan. What Jeremiah sensed God was saying was quite different: yes, deliverance would come, but not yet. So his advice was that the people settle down and find God where they were.

Often we find ourselves in times of waiting and looking for God's dramatic touch upon our lives. There is nothing wrong with that, but our calling is that no matter what we are waiting for, we need to look for him in the here and now as well. If we always focus on what God is going to do in the future, we run the real risk of missing him now.

When people come to our Healing Mission for prayer, the approach we often take is to ask them where Jesus is for them right now – not where would they like him to be, but where he is in the here and now.

Take a moment to find a place of quiet, and in the stillness ask the same question, "Where is Jesus for me right now?" What comes to mind? Engage with him and find his presence.

Living for his glory

> *In him we were also chosen… in order that we …might be for the praise of his glory.*
> **Ephesians 1.11–12**

This verse reveals Paul's dream for other people to look at us and see something so wonderful about God that they turn to him in praise. Now that really is something to live up to! It is true that people do look at us, but what is it they really see? It can be quite a frightening thought! The temptation is to think that we have to do something for people to see God in us, that we have to act in a particularly holy way, or put on a spiritual mask, but this is not what Paul is saying.

Instead, it all hinges on what God does, and not on what we have to do. Paul is suggesting that God's presence within us is natural, simply because we bear his mark upon us. So is there anything we have to do?

Perhaps what is required of us is to believe it. Spend just two or three minutes letting these words, 'I bear your name, O LORD God Almighty' (Jeremiah 15.16), run through your mind. Holding on to this truth is what opens the door for God's presence and naturalness to flow through us, and is what will make the difference to those around us.

> ‘ *If any of you lacks wisdom, he should ask God...* ’
>
> **James 1.5**

Listening to God | 1

This verse makes it sound so simple: we want God to speak to us so all we have to do is to ask him. Yet how many people read these words with some dejection? Have we not all had moments when we have called out to God and he has not answered? How can it be this simple? Perhaps another way of looking at this is that God does indeed speak to us, but we do not always recognise his voice.

How do we expect God to speak to us? In a deep thundering voice or by writing on a wall? In the much loved passage from 1 Kings 19, Elijah hears the voice of God in 'a gentle whisper' (verse 12). A whisper is as real as an earthquake, but it is very easy to overlook, and that is perhaps what so many of us do.

So the voice of God may come to us like a whisper, or as a spontaneous thought or a picture that suddenly appears in our minds. Maybe God is speaking to us all the time, but we simply don't believe that it is God. Of course, we have to test these things, but testing comes after we have received; it is not an outright dismissal.

Take a moment to ask God to whisper what he thinks of you. Pay attention to the whisper, and enjoy his presence.

The God who does not find fault | 2

' If any of you lacks wisdom, he should ask God, who gives generously to all without finding fault...'

James 1.5

If we ask God to speak to us, many of us will assume that he wants to say something harsh or condemning, and that more than likely it will probably be about our sin! Perhaps that is why so many people are rather reluctant to listen to God; they are not sure they want to hear what they think he will say!

These are probably some of the most releasing words in the Bible, and are wonderfully reassuring: we come to a generous God who does not find fault with us. This is the confidence that Hebrews 4 speaks about when it says that we can approach the throne of grace 'with confidence'. It is with this confidence that we will find acceptance and love, not fault-finding or criticism.

As you begin to pray today, sit quietly before God before you utter any intercessions for other people. Slowly repeat over and over, "God gives generously without finding fault." As you say these words and the conviction of them grows within you, you may begin to find a new confidence in coming before the throne of grace – and the peace of God will begin to flood your heart.

Banish the sharks! | 3

> *But when he asks, he must believe and not doubt, because he who doubts is like a wave of the sea, blown and tossed by the wind.*
>
> **James 1.6**

What is it that we must believe in and not doubt? Is this one of those verses that is asking us to believe we have something that we plainly do not have?

Perhaps one of the main things we are asked to hold on to here is linked to the previous verse, which we have already looked at: namely, that God is generous and does not find fault in us.

It is a common experience for many of us to dip our toes into the waters of God's love only to see 'sharks' swimming around, so we hastily jump back onto dry land. These sharks are the voices of the one the Bible calls 'the thief', who loves to plunder the things of God (John 10.10). The voice of the thief comes in the form of accusation: "How can these things apply to you with all that you have done wrong?"; "How could he love you that much? No one else does." The question is whose voice will we listen to? To the whisper of God, who is generous and does not find fault, or to the sneers of the one who would seek to rob us of all that God has for us?

As you sit before God now, recognise the efforts of the thief to distract you, and fix your attention instead upon Almighty God, who loves you and is calling you to a new life with him.

Finding God's passion in our actions

The zeal of the LORD Almighty will accomplish this.

Isaiah 9.7

In chapter 9, Isaiah talks about a list of beautiful things that we would all love to see established, including the rule and reign of God and his justice over all. In this verse he talks about the 'how', which is the passionate desire of God to bring all of this about.

This does not mean, of course, that we can sit back and watch God do all the work, as we, too, have a part to play; Paul talks about us being 'God's fellow-workers' (1 Corinthians 3.9). However, our efforts – whether it is doing something on a global scale to rectify injustice or reflecting God's heart to a lonely person – all take on a different perspective when we see behind them the zeal of the Lord and his passionate desire for his people.

Having that vision of God's heart behind everything we do changes our perspective on our actions. No longer are they simply duties that we must undertake, but rather they are our response to the passions of God. This is his longing for us.

Whatever we do today in his name, whether it seems to be a big thing for God or a simple act of kindness to another person, let us pause and seek to catch God's passion for what we do.

> '...his love
> endures
> for ever.'

1 Chronicles 16.34

The continuous thread of love

Phrases like this can often trip off the tongue without us really grasping the wonder of what they mean. It sounds like a poetic statement, a general truth, but actually it says something incredibly wonderful to us.

God's constant love is an amazing concept: that there is a continuous thread of God's love woven through eternity, and therefore woven through our lives. If we look back over our lives, the thread of his love has been there. Actually, it is far easier to see God's love as we look back than as we face today or the future, but the challenge for us is to believe that the chord of his love will be there in the future, and perhaps especially it will be there today.

We all have some notion of what this day will bring: there will be things we are looking forward to and some moments of anxiety. Through every part of this day the chord of God's love has already been woven. It is there; it goes before us. Spend a few moments now letting these wonderful words sink in and then, as the day unfolds, consciously bring them back to mind so that the vision of the thread of God's love in your life becomes visible.

He's for real

' Jesus declared, "I who speak to you am he."'

John 4.26

The context of this statement is that Jesus is speaking to a Samaritan woman, and she is trying to grasp the significance of what he is saying. She declares that she is waiting for the Messiah, who will make everything clear. At this point Jesus speaks these powerful words, "I who speak to you am he", and declares himself to be the Messiah. If she believes what he says to be true, presumably everything else he says can be trusted.

This is a conviction to which we all need to return, for there will be many moments when things around us are confusing and life is not working out as we would like. At moments like this, do we trust the words of Jesus that he will be with us always? If what he says is right and he is here with us, then he must be present, with all his compassion and power, to help us. If that is so, then our fears will subside. However, this will only be the case if we really trust this statement from John 4 – that Jesus really is who he says he is.

Find a quiet place and let your plans for the day go through your mind, or if your present moment is a moment of panic, be honest about that. Let the words of Jesus,"I am with you always", settle over you and your plans or still the panic within you. Slowly repeat these words and let his presence change your outlook.

Coming to God

> "My people have committed two sins: They have forsaken me, the spring of living water, and have dug their own cisterns, broken cisterns that cannot hold water."
>
> **Jeremiah 2.13**

The sadness that God seeks to convey through this verse in Jeremiah is that God's people have taken their eyes off God and started to seek in other things what they could find in him.

Let's take a moment to see the incredible good news in this statement: God is saying that he can be everything to us. If we are honest, we would probably say that we are all too aware of using other people, or even things, to support us and comfort us. There isn't actually anything wrong in this, as God gave us each other for our mutual support, and creation is there to be enjoyed. However, when we turn to these people or things before we turn to God, we get it the wrong way round. God will comfort us through other people, but if we seek their comfort before we turn to him, we run the risk of being described as those people who dig their own cisterns.

God delights in his children bringing their needs to him and he is well aware of the love and comfort that we need. He is not asking us to forego such comfort, but he is longing for us to come to him more and more with our needs. In this way we will see more clearly our dependence on him and his joy in our presence.

Bearing
his name | 1

The Bible contains many titles or names of God, and each of them reveal something special about his character. Simply speaking, each name is a reminder of some aspect of God that can be instilled in us. As we look at some of these names over the next week, let's capture the wonder of Jesus, and all that he is, living in us through his Holy Spirit.

Paul writes in Colossians 1.19 that 'God was pleased to have all his fullness dwell in him [Jesus]'. The amazing truth is that if the fullness of God dwells in Jesus, and Jesus dwells in us, then we also have all the fullness of God dwelling in us. Everything that was in Jesus – his peace, patience, kindness and love, as well as all his power and might – is also in us.

As we begin to ponder some of the titles for God over these next few days, be aware that they are not simply words, but names for what also dwells in us; names that reveal a resource to which we have access because of the truth that Jesus dwells in us through the Holy Spirit.

As you spend a few moments with God now, let these words touch you: 'All the fullness of God is living in me.' Enjoy them, and let them enrich you.

The Lord is
my provider | 2

When Abraham named the place where he almost sacrificed his son 'The LORD Will Provide', he set down a marker for something he had discovered to be true, and he wanted everyone to know the truth as strongly as he did. The circumstances of the story of Abraham's willingness to sacrifice Isaac are well known and in many ways it seems a barbaric story, but this lesson about God's provision is one that Abraham would never forget, and the place, "The LORD Will Provide", is a place for us to take to heart as well.

The truth that God is our provider echoes through the Bible. It is one of the names of God that people through the ages have found be true, and is a truth to which Jesus often returned, assuring his followers that if God provides for the birds of the air, surely he will care for them since they are of more value than the birds.

We all have different needs, whether physical, spiritual, emotional or social, and it is encouraging that one of the first names God reveals about himself in the Bible is that of provider. There is nothing wrong in having needs, but the way in which we give voice to them is important. We shouldn't express our needs out of helplessness or despair, but rather bring them to God, who has declared that he wants to be known as the one who provides.

We bear his name, 'Provider', and every time a need arises within us we can carry his name to this need. Say "The LORD Will Provide" to yourself for a few minutes and come back to it again throughout the day.

The Lord is my banner | 3

'The LORD is my Banner'

Exodus 17.15

Exodus 17 tells the wonderful story of when Moses defeated the Amalekites, a victory that was won both by Joshua's skills on the battlefield and by Moses raising his hands to heaven as he stood on the mountain above.

In verse 9, we read that it was not just his hands that Moses raised, but the staff he held in them. It was the same staff that had turned into a snake as a sign of God's presence with him, and the same staff with which he had struck the Nile and turned it to blood. When he struck the ground with his staff, the dust became gnats, and as he raised his staff over the sea the waters parted.

It is not that the staff was anything magical, but rather that it had come to represent the power of God. When Moses felt it in his hands, it must have encouraged him to believe God could do anything. When he named the place where he built an altar, 'The LORD is my Banner', he was calling everyone to remember that God is faithful, and that by holding on to him we will have the victory.

You may not have a staff, but you do have the cross. This is what you can lift up in your times of difficulty: let it represent the love of God that sent Jesus to you, the power of God over sin and the weapon God used to overcome the works of the devil.

As you sit in God's presence, hold a cross if you have one. Let it be a reminder that there is no limit to his love for you, no work of the devil that can stand against him and nothing that cannot be rectified by his power.

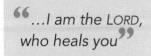

> **❝**...I am the LORD,
> who heals you**❞**

Exodus 15.26

The Lord is
our healer | 4

Despite all the medical progress over the years and our fascination and preoccupation with health and fitness, the word 'healing' continues to attract and draw us to seek something we need.

Perhaps it is because people are less frightened to admit to issues such as stress or even aspects of mental illness, but certainly the need for healing seems to be as great as it ever was. So this revelation of God as our healer resonates with us all and says two profound things.

The first thing it says is that God is on the side of those who are weak. The very name 'healer' implies a deep care for those who are in need of healing. If you feel that describes you, you already have God's attention.

The second thing it says is that God is seeking to bring change to those of us who are in need. God does not simply sympathise, he is our 'healer' and we can seek him as such.

The healing God brings can come in a variety of ways. Most commonly, it seems to flow through others to us. A massive step to finding God's healing is to summon up the courage to ask someone to pray for you. These prayers may be profound or they may be simple, but they are in accord with this revelation of God as the one who wants to be known as our healer.

Which part of your life do you want to offer to Christ the healer right now? What do you need him to do for you that you cannot do for yourself?

The Lord is peace | 5

'The LORD is Peace.'
Judges 6.24

When Gideon meets an angel of the Lord (it may even be the Lord himself), his understanding is that to be in such close proximity to God is to die. Yet after this meeting, God speaks the word 'peace' to Gideon and assures him that he is not going to die. In relief and thanksgiving, Gideon names the place where this encounter took place, 'The LORD is Peace'.

The wonderful truth revealed in this passage is that God's desire is to speak peace to us. Of all the things we imagine God might want to say to us, peace is probably not the first. We often imagine him wanting to have a word with us about our sins and failings – perhaps because we are so aware of them that our assumption is that God must be as well.

What is so revealing about this name of God is that it shows us that God does not simply give peace, he *is* peace. Peace is at the very core of his being.

As a bearer of his name, you can expect to experience the wonder of God's peace in your life, not as a result of anything you have achieved but as a consequence of who he is. As you sit quietly now, find the peace that God brings and take it with you into the hours ahead.

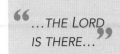

Seated
on high | 6

Whenever we ask ourselves the question, 'Where is Jesus?', the truth is that there is more than one answer.

On the one hand Jesus is always with us; he has made his home within us and it is his pleasure to dwell in us. Yet it is equally true that at the same time he is also seated at the right hand of the Father in heaven, in glory with all things beneath his feet.

That is what we are reminded of in the last words of the book of Ezekiel. The prophet describes the heavenly city and concludes the description by revealing the name of it: "THE LORD IS THERE".

When your problems seem too big for you, you need to begin to see them from the perspective of the one who is seated above all things, as this changes your perception of them. He is the Lord, and the problems are not lording it over him.

You bear his name. You bear the truth and the reality of the one who is Lord over all. You carry this truth into every situation into which you walk. Take a moment to hold the hours ahead in your mind, and over each event and situation have this assurance: the Lord is there.

You are righteous | 7

The final title we are looking at in this series is one that occurs twice in the book of Jeremiah. It is a name of God that is a constant reminder of both our need for him and the promise of hope that is with us at all times.

One of the central facts of our faith is that Jesus died for our sins. We are not in a position to do anything about our past, but he is. In fact, he has done something about it already – he has paid for our sins and therefore declared us to be innocent and righteous (right) in his eyes. No matter what we may see when we look in the mirror, when he looks at us he sees people that he has declared free.

This is the liberating hope in which we live: whatever we think may stand against us, Jesus sees us as being free because of what he has done.

So much energy can go into revisiting our past and so much time can be spent in regret, but regret changes nothing. The only thing that can change us is by facing the truth that Jesus has declared us forgiven and free.

This is the truth you bear within you wherever you go or whatever you have done: because of what Jesus has done, you are righteous. He stamps forgiveness upon every sin you think stands against you.

> *'You shall not misuse the name of the LORD your God...'*
>
> **Deuteronomy 5.11**

Misusing the name of God

We rightly apply this command to things such as swearing and uttering inappropriate oaths, although there may be another application of this commandment that is both challenging and awesome.

Jeremiah 15.16 states, 'I bear your name, O LORD God Almighty.' Jeremiah's words are later developed by Paul, who explains that our bodies are dwelling places for the presence of God.

Perhaps one of our greatest misuses of the name of God is by having little or no awareness of his presence within us. Either we assume that Jeremiah's claim is not true for us or we forget to tune into it throughout the day. The challenge of this command in Deuteronomy is to find ways of remembering his presence with us. Let the words of Jeremiah, 'I bear your name, O LORD God Almighty', be true for you. Dare to believe you really are carrying the Lord's presence within you at all times.

Doing good

> *'Anyone, then, who knows the good he ought to do and doesn't do it, sins.'*
> **James 4.17**

We may think we have a pretty good idea of what makes something a sin, and could come up with a list of actions we would be able to identify by that word. However, this verse from James presents a whole new challenge with regard to the concept of sin. It is not just about the bad things we do, but also the good things we don't do.

Fortunately, there is a very positive side to this. It is the invitation for all of us to ask the question, "What good can I do?" at the beginning of each day and as we go through our daily lives.

You may not think of yourself as a particularly influential person; your life may seem quite ordinary in comparison to other people. Yet the reality is that you will probably come into contact with any number of people today, either by chance encounter or by planned meetings. It is said that every contact leaves a trace; what trace do you want to leave with the contacts you make today?

It begins by believing that this applies to us. Today you can help to make a difference to someone's hour, day or even their life.

Jesus is praying for us

In this passage Peter is about to be told that he is going to fail Jesus, despite his protestations to the contrary. That news is preceded by these words spoken by Jesus. They must have brought such comfort to Peter after the event; Jesus had already spoken to his 'Abba Father' about the situation.

What was true of Peter is also true of each one of us. Jesus has prayed for us, he has spoken to his 'Abba Father' about us. In Romans 8.34, Paul reveals a vision of Jesus seated at the right hand of God interceding, or praying, for us. The context in which Paul writes is very personal. He has just been speaking about the people who have been called by God. That includes us, and Jesus is praying for each one of us.

All too often we do not pray as we think we should. Our prayers may seem weak and faithless. However, things do not depend on our prayers alone. We have Jesus, who is seated close to God and who is bringing our needs and cares to his (and our) Abba Father. If nothing else gives us hope, this revelation should. At this very moment in time, Jesus is praying for you.

The God who sees me

> 'She gave this name to the LORD who spoke to her: "You are the God who sees me."'
>
> **Genesis 16.13**

If God really is everywhere all the time, of course he sees everything, but what do we think God really sees? It is our answer to that question that probably reveals something about the nature of our relationship with God.

Many people are convinced that what God sees most of all is our sin. We assume this is what God looks at, because it is often what we are most aware of. The story of Hagar in this chapter of Genesis is illuminating. Hagar's attitude to Sarah was probably the cause of her plight: Sarah realised that Hagar despised her and began to mistreat her. Hagar fled to the desert, where God saw her and spoke to her. As a result, Hagar's name for God was, 'You are the God who sees me.'

It is interesting that when God speaks to Hagar, it isn't about her attitude, which had probably caused the situation in the first place. What he speaks about is what he sees of her potential and her future.

Our God is a God who sees, but don't assume that all he is interested in are your woes and failings. He sees your dreams for your life, and his dreams for your life. He sees who you are and what has happened to you and, most importantly, he loves what he sees.

Spend time with him right now, resting in his presence, no matter how near or far you feel from him – he is there, looking at you and loving you.

You matter

And Abraham said to God, "If only Ishmael might live under your blessing!"

Genesis 17.18

Abraham uttered these words in response to God's extraordinary promise that he and Sarah would have a child, and that through this child a great nation would be born. Given their advancing years and the fact that Sarah had been unable to conceive in the past, Abraham was naturally challenged by the promise. He wonders if a simpler solution might be for God to carry out his promise in a different way – through someone else, such as Ishmael – but God is determined to do it his way.

We are all children of promise. God has promised us that his presence and his intervention will go with us through life. We just have a hard time believing it! We often assume that God will take easy options, such as use someone else, when in reality he wants to use us.

God's commitment to us personally is perhaps one of the hardest things for us to grasp. He loves the whole world, but he also loves you individually. He has many people he could use to bring about his purposes, but he wants to use you specifically. He has a grand plan for the whole world, and he has a plan for you personally.

You are unique, individually gifted, and personally called to be a means through whom God desires to bless others. You matter to God, and you make a difference to his world.

The right to be a child of God

> 'Yet to all who received him, to those who believed in his name, he gave the right to become children of God'
>
> **John 1.12**

This beautiful verse emphasises that no matter who we are or what our background is, every single one of us has the privilege to come to God as Abba, Father.

Of course, we could all be more open and committed – there is always more we can do – but once we have made that step towards Jesus and opened our hearts to him, so much more is given to us: the right to see ourselves as children of God and call ourselves as such.

As if that wasn't enough, our right to call God 'Father' is wonderfully linked to our relationship with Jesus, in that we are invited to have the same relationship with our Father that Jesus had. When Jesus was praying (John 17.26), he spoke to his Father about the love they both shared also being in us. Jesus' prayer, or desire, was that the love he and the Father enjoyed might be the love that we enjoy.

This is your privilege, your calling and your right. You can step into this relationship right now; it is meant for you. There is nothing more God can do to bring it about. He is waiting for you to enjoy it. Begin to accept the truth of these words, 'You are my Father, and I belong to you.'

You are wonderful!

> *...I am fearfully and wonderfully made; your works are wonderful*
>
> **Psalm 139.14**

Most people have a fairly poor impression of themselves, either because they feel bad about past actions or because other people have told them directly, or given the impression, that they are of little value.

We can easily end up comparing ourselves to other people, and usually we find ourselves lacking in some significant way. This statement stands against that and shouts out something totally different – that we are wonderful in the eyes of God.

These words invite us to proclaim something that we grudgingly must know is true – namely that God never creates something sub-standard; what he creates has his touch upon it. We are his creation and we bear the mark of his hands upon us.

As we ponder the wonder of who we are, perhaps the area needing most reflection is the fact that we are temples of his Holy Spirit, we carry him within us wherever we go and whatever we do; we are individually and uniquely marked with the presence of God.

You may look at yourself and wonder what God sees in you. You may well compare yourself to others, but when God looks at you, what he sees is the wonder of his presence in you. Spend a moment catching the implication of this incredible truth.

Overcoming timidity

What could God do through you today? If it is true that a spirit of power and love is within us, what difference can we make to those

> *For God did not give us a spirit of timidity, but a spirit of power, of love and of self-discipline.*
>
> **2 Timothy 1.7**

people we will meet today? The answer, of course, is we can make a big difference, but other things hold us back.

It is with a spirit of self-discipline that we need to attack the timidity that so often grips us. We may dream dreams of what God could do through us; we may have an awareness of the presence of God within us; and we will probably find ourselves in situations where the thought goes through our minds to say something, or offer to pray for someone – but we draw back, wondering what people will think of us, or suddenly overcome by the thought that we may have got it wrong.

Self-discipline is not just about the discipline to lead a good life; it is not just about saying 'no' to temptation, it is also about saying 'no' to timidity and fear. So what if we haven't got it wrong and the Spirit is prompting us and nudging us? What if the power of God could do something wonderful in those situations?

This is a verse worth memorising and carrying into the day ahead, so that whenever feelings of timidity rise up you can bring these words to mind. Then maybe you really can let him work through you.

The gentleness of Jesus

When Isaiah saw into the future, he glimpsed something of the coming Messiah. This verse reveals that he saw something beautiful about Jesus, namely that he would be so gentle and tender to those he came to save.

We all need more and more of Jesus, yet what often stops us coming to him is fear – the fear that he may turn us away because of what we have done or that he will be disappointed in us in some way.

The revelation that gentleness and tenderness are the hallmarks of Jesus' character is recorded precisely so that we can trust these words; it is safe to come to him. If we are bruised, he will not break us; if the fire within us has almost gone out, he will not extinguish it.

Perhaps you feel bruised by any number of things as you come before Jesus today. There may be things you want to bring to him, some personal or painful. With all that is on your heart, come to Jesus, who is revealed to be gentle and tender and is waiting for you to come to him.

Repaying evil

The six simple words in this verse contain so much wisdom. At the heart of it, a practical application would be: if someone does something bad to you, don't do something bad in return. It is interesting to note that this is a command; it is something that we are to obey, and there is good news and bad news that accompany it!

The good news is that presumably we can obey this commandment; it is actually possible to put it into practice. It would be unbearably harsh to be told to obey something we were unable to do. The reason we are able to do this is because God has poured into our hearts the Spirit of Jesus. This is the same Jesus who prayed for the forgiveness of the men who were killing him. The Spirit that was in him is the same Spirit that is in us.

The bad news is that we will at various points, in differing degrees, have opportunities to put this command into practice. Things will happen to all of us that will cause us to want to react in a way that is probably not of God. However, we do have a choice: because of the Holy Spirit within us we can choose to pause, and rather than react badly to the situation we can act in accordance with the power that God has put within us.

As you face the events of the day ahead, perhaps you know there are going to be moments when there is a real chance you will react in a negative manner. It might help to think about this in advance, and as you do so recall that the same Spirit who was in Jesus is also in you.

Friendship

The beginning of Genesis is an incredible picture of God's creation and the rebellion of the human race against him. It is not just about the fall of Adam and Eve in the garden; within a few chapters, human beings are described as corrupt and violent (verses 11–13). In contrast, two people, Enoch and Noah, stand out. Both are described as men who walked with God (Genesis 5.24 and 6.9). What a beautiful aspiration for us – to be people who walk with God, people who are God's friends.

One of the characteristics of a friend of God is someone who does not treat prayer as something that is only done at set times of the day. Instead, there is an ongoing awareness and conversation with God, and an honesty about friendship. We can talk to God about anything that bothers us, be it big or small. We can talk about our weaknesses and temptations, and the more we do so the less of a mask we put up and the more intimate we become with him.

Friends also listen to each other. Just as we can pour out our hearts to God and know he listens, so we can expect him to speak to us. As you read the Bible, catch his heart in the words you read and expect him to speak – often as random thoughts or Bible verses that come into your mind. The desire to be intimate with God is all it takes for you to sow seeds of this friendship into your life. As you sit with God now, see him as a friend. What you ought to say is not important, it's being with him that counts.

God has not given up on us

There is something incredibly hopeful about this detail from the story of Jesus healing a man at the pool of Bethesda. It probably strikes you that if someone had been in such a dire condition for 38 years, it would be natural to assume that not much was going to change. That was not what struck Jesus. The man may well have been there for a long time, but that did not mean he had to stay in misery.

> 'One who was there had been an invalid for thirty-eight years. When Jesus saw him lying there and learned that he had been in this condition for a long time, he asked him, "Do you want to get well?"'
> **John 5.5–6**

What this account says to us is that no matter who we are, and no matter how long we have been suffering, God has not forgotten us. Nor are we right to assume that just because we have been suffering for a long time there is no more hope of help from God. So how do we approach God when our condition is long-standing?

Perhaps one of the main things we can hold on to is the fact that Jesus is with us. In this story, Jesus was in the place where those in need gathered. Similarly, he is with us and is not embarrassed by us. When we pray, his attitude is not one of, "Not you again!" When we come to him today, he is there for us, just as he was the first time we ever approached him.

Be yourself with Jesus today; you don't need to hide anything from him. He is with you anyway, and knows you through and through.

> *Before I formed you in the womb I knew you, before you were born I set you apart.*
>
> **Jeremiah 1.5**

Being utterly known

I wonder what Jeremiah thought when he heard God speaking these words to him? It must have startled him. Presumably he assumed he was going about his own business like everyone else. If he did think about God, it was probably more to do with trying to please him and not to sin too much – and then God reveals this stunning truth that actually he has been intimately involved in Jeremiah's whole being since before the womb! Even back then, Jeremiah had been chosen and appointed by God. How amazing Jeremiah would have felt.

All that is true of Jeremiah is true of us. Just as Jeremiah was known to God before his physical life took shape, so were we; just as he was appointed to his calling, so are we.

Psalm 139.13 speaks about us being knit together in our mothers' wombs. Ephesians 1.4 speaks about us being chosen before the foundation of the world. What changed Jeremiah is when he heard God speak it to him personally. Why not let the Spirit do that for you?

Sit in the quiet for a few minutes and let the Father speak these words to you: "Before I formed you in the womb I knew you, before you were born I set you apart." Repeat them slowly to yourself and catch the wonder of what you mean to God.

What do you want?

The woman saw how beautiful the tree was and how good its fruit would be to eat, and she thought how wonderful it would be to become wise.

Genesis 3.6 (GNB)

This extract is how the Good News Bible translates Eve's wonder as she stared at the forbidden fruit in the Garden of Eden. In her case, the word she ended this sentence with was 'wise', but it is possible we could all put a word in at the end of the sentence to describe something that we really want: "How wonderful it would be to become…". If we are honest enough to do that, it might reveal something about the desires of our hearts. What might your word be – wise, powerful, wealthy, attractive?

In his letter, James speaks about the desires that battle within us (James 4.1–3). The desires are there, we just don't really like them, and so we probably pretend they are not there in the first place. What James advocates is that we admit these desires and actually ask God for them, presumably because if we do not ask God for them we are going to be tempted to get them by other means.

There is, however, a small catch! James warns against using what we have for our own pleasures. When God gives, it is a gift of love, but a gift he loves to be shared. The power that God gives is a power to minister to others, the wealth that God gives is a wealth that he wants shared and the wisdom God gives is wisdom that he wants to be used for service. So God loves to give, but he loves what he gives to be used to bless others as well as ourselves. What is your heart's desire? Rather than hide it, bring it in to his glorious light.

God, the glorious shepherd | 1

This is one of those beautiful phrases in the Bible that can have a growing influence upon us as we put a different emphasis on different words.

The Lord is our shepherd. He is none other than the creator of heaven and earth, the one who planned creation, the one who called Abraham and Moses, who stands before us and guides us. It is an incredible truth that the Lord upon whom we call is the same God who parted the Red Sea, who provided food for the Israelites and who, through Jesus, opened the eyes of the blind and called the dead from the tombs.

Whenever we read the Bible, it is always worth asking, what does this passage say about the God who is my God? It is so often true that our perception of God is too small, and this affects the faith we have in his ability or willingness to be there for us. This is one reason why worship is so important. Worship lifts our vision of the one to whom we pray to new levels, reminds us of who he is and brings us back to the truth that it is the Lord God himself who is our shepherd.

As you come to God this day, begin by seeking to catch a bigger vision of him. Perhaps remind yourself slowly of some of the many names by which God is called in the Bible. Recall as many as you can, or look back over them again (pp24–30). Our God is all of these.

The Lord is my shepherd | 2

'The LORD is my shepherd'

Psalm 23.1

Something special happens when we can make the transition from God being 'God' to being 'my God'. When we are able to speak to God in these personal terms, it is not that we in any way own him or have any control over him, but rather that we recognise his lordship over us and his love for us personally. In a very beautiful moment in the account of the resurrection in John's Gospel, Jesus says to Mary, "I am returning to my Father and your Father, to my God and your God" (John 20.17). Jesus is encouraging us to take seriously the fact that God is there, not just for the whole world, but for each of us personally.

This reality is something we probably need to come back to many times over the course of a day; that God delights in us personally, feels for us personally, cares for us personally and will therefore guide us personally like a shepherd. If you choose to believe this, what you are doing is letting what is real become true for you. He is your God and nothing can change this, but when you acknowledge this truth and let him truly be your God, you open the door for him to act in your life in a new and fresh way.

What does a shepherd do? | 3

If you live in a town or city, the notion of a shepherd may not mean much to you; you may not meet many shepherds in the course of your day! However, the concept of a shepherd is an analogy to which the Bible returns quite a few times. In a wonderful moment in John's Gospel, Jesus refers to himself as the good shepherd (John 10.11).

Another key passage in the Bible for understanding the relevance of shepherds is Ezekiel 34. In this chapter, the leaders of the people are seen as bad shepherds and they stand in contrast to God, the ultimate good shepherd. The difference between their leadership and God's shepherding is seen at the beginning of the chapter when they are compared to God in this way: "You have not strengthened the weak or healed the sick or bound up the injured. You have not brought back the strays or searched for the lost" (Ezekiel 34.4). The stress here is that the bad shepherds did not undertake any of these duties, yet they are precisely the things that God does in our lives.

The Bible states that God is our shepherd, and Jesus reiterated this about himself. As you come to God today, consider him as your good shepherd. He loves to strengthen you when you are weak, heal you when you are sick, comfort you when you are bruised by life and bring you back when you have wandered.

Being watched | 4

This is a beautiful promise that, if we think about it, is very bold: we will never be in want. The rest of the psalm goes on to explain the nature of God's provision for us. In this verse, however, a wonderful truth is revealed, namely that we have a God who provides for us.

If we are in need, and whatever the nature of that need, we must first understand the reason why we will not lack anything. God, who has committed himself to being our living Lord in a personal way, has also committed himself to being not just a God who reigns in heaven but also a shepherd who walks by our side as we move though life; he provides for us along the way.

This is one of the most extraordinary truths about our faith: that our Lord is the same Lord who reigns in heaven and looks down on creation with all the authority of heaven, and yet at the same time he walks with us through this life, watching over us and caring for us.

Today he is watching over you and standing by you every step along the way.

> *He makes me lie down in green pastures, he leads me beside quiet waters...*
>
> **Psalm 23.2**

Being at peace | 5

Green pastures and quiet waters are external images of something internal to which we probably all aspire: peace. The words in this verse speak of a tranquillity for which our often hurt and broken lives long. But there are two interesting points about this tranquillity.

The first is that peace and tranquillity are directly linked to following the shepherd. They are not feelings that come upon us as we pursue our own means of finding them; they come as we follow the one whom the Bible calls 'The Prince of Peace'. The peace that is promised to us is real and very beautiful, but it is not of our own making. It comes from God.

The second point to note is that if this peace comes through following the shepherd, we need to recognise the importance of following him, because we probably would not find the path ourselves. In other words, the path to peace along which the shepherd chooses to take us may not be a path we would ordinarily choose to take. It may involve what we see as hardship and seeming danger and insecurity. Yet if we are seeking to follow the shepherd, the destination will be beautiful and we will always have someone with us to help us.

Peace is something we all desire and it is good to express this desire to God, but as you do so place this day in his hands, trust him with it and let him lead you to the peaceful path.

Coming to
the shepherd | 6

There is a saying that time is a great healer. It may take away the immediacy of our pain, but it rarely removes it altogether. Our healer and our restorer is not time, but Jesus, who loves us and gave himself for us. This healing and restoring begins by us knowing our need of him. So many times we read in the Gospels that the people who were healed by Jesus were those who actually came to him, the ones who stepped out of the crowd and fell at his feet.

The pain we bear is real. It may be the memory of people we have lost, the pain of rejection or loss or of missed opportunities or seemingly wasted years.

This psalm states that there is the hope of restoration, and that hope comes from Jesus. The same Jesus who healed the sick and forgave sinners is the one who promises to restore us. This restoration does not come with the passing of time, but by encountering Jesus and letting something of his healing touch reach out to us.

Whatever your pains, make a conscious decision not to bury them away deep inside, but to own up to them with honesty and bring them to Jesus, who promises to restore you. Take a step to begin to do this right now.

> 'He guides me in paths of righteousness for his name's sake.'
>
> **Psalm 23.3**

Receiving guidance | 7

There are two aspects to guidance, both of which tell us much about God's love and tenderness towards us. The first is that he does indeed guide us along certain paths. That guidance can come in several ways. It may be what we call 'coincidence' (which some people prefer to call 'God-incidence'), it may be the gentle nudge that we feel within us or it may be the wise words of a friend. Often we know exactly what God wants for us, we are just not sure we want to do it! However it comes, this is our loving Father nudging us along certain paths that he knows will be good for us.

The second aspect his guiding love reveals is that we are not robots programmed to perform in certain ways and go in set directions. God loves us for our individuality, and we are able to choose whether to follow his guidance or to take another path. Of course, we will always do better to follow his guidance, but if we choose not to, he will still be there seeking to guide us back. He certainly won't stop loving us if we wander from the path.

Paul encourages us to offer our bodies as a living sacrifice to God (Romans 12.1); in other words, to seek his guidance and follow it willingly. He will love us anyway, but our offerings are sweet and pleasant to him. Our response to him can bring him pleasure.

What guidance are you seeking for your life, or for this day? Be still and listen for his voice.

Thorns as well as roses | 8

Even though I walk through the valley of the shadow of death...

Psalm 23.4

If only it were true that as soon as we set our hearts to follow God, life would turn out to be a perpetual bed of roses. Sadly we know that this is not true. Many times in our Christian lives we walk along paths that we feel we should be protected from, paths that frankly confuse us. What can really hurt even more is when people assume that because we are going through hard times we must have done something wrong, and their suggestion is that what we really need to do is to confess something that they are pretty certain is lurking there somewhere!

If you feel that this describes you, let this verse bring you comfort. Even the sheep being guided by the shepherd, who knew where the pastures and still waters were, at times also had to walk through very dark valleys.

This was certainly true of Jesus, who was tempted, misunderstood, falsely accused and surrounded by friends who didn't understand – and that is before we take the cross into consideration. In his times of fellowship with his Father, and as he rested with his friends, he understood the pastures; at other times the valleys probably seemed very deep. We, like him, are not immune from the valleys, but we are still OK, still loved by God and he still takes pleasure in us.

> *...I will fear no evil, for you are with me*
>
> **Psalm 23.4**

Dealing with fear | 9

Fear can be a natural response to a situation over which we feel we have no control. It may be entirely rational or completely irrational. To simply tell someone not to fear is not really very helpful. Fear is removed when it is replaced by something else – in this case, the confidence that someone greater than what we fear is present.

The potential for fear in this psalm is very great. David has just spoken about walking through a valley of the shadow of death, yet he will not fear because he is certain that the shepherd is with him.

Our particular fears might be very real, but so is Jesus. Our problems occur when we let the presence of our fears dislodge the presence of Jesus, and then do nothing about it. Practise finding Jesus in the times of peace, and then in times of fear you will be able to call upon the greatest resource you have.

If this is a time of fear or confusion, find Jesus now. Remind yourself of God's amazing, perfect love, a love so great that he sent Jesus for you. Now ask yourself where Jesus is for you and seek his presence. Let his presence be a greater presence than the situation or person that you fear.

The weapon of worship | 10

'...your rod and your staff, they comfort me.'

Psalm 23.4

The presence of Jesus with us is not simply a nice feeling that can bring reassurance. This is the presence of the one who stilled a storm. When we find the presence of Jesus with us, or when we have that sense of his assurance, it is worth asking what we expect him to do now that he is here? Sometimes we may have a strange notion that he will stand by and watch bad things happen to us because he knows it will ultimately be good for us, which is not true.

As David walked through that valley of the shadow of death, he knew that the shepherd was with him and was actively looking after him, using his rod and staff on his behalf. In fact, simply being aware that the shepherd had a staff was of comfort to David in his perilous walk.

The Jesus who walks with us in our fears is the same Jesus who is seated at the right hand of God and is Lord over all. The weapon we have is that of worship. As we acknowledge Jesus for who he is, for his presence with us, for his Lordship over everything, the reality of his powerful presence becomes even more real. He walks with us; his active love for us is a reality. Let's expect to see him work on our behalf.

> 'You prepare a table before me in the presence of my enemies.'
>
> **Psalm 23.5**

The rough and the smooth | 11

What is wonderful about this particular verse is that it brings together two realities that we find so hard to combine in our lives. On the one hand it speaks about the reality of God's goodness, his pleasure and provision for us, and on the other hand it speaks about our enemies – the people or situations that seem to conspire against us.

We may well have had experience of both. There have probably been times when we can look back and see the Lord's hand upon our lives, and yet we also know the reality of darker times, when nothing seems to go right and forces seem to conspire against us.

What is wonderful about this phrase is that David puts the two together. When our enemies are present, so is the Lord. Too often we equate difficulty with God's absence or with his displeasure. Such a divide is simply not true.

At the end of the day, or at the beginning of the next, look back and acknowledge the difficulties – what was hard, why did you feel so attacked or rejected? Then call to mind the times of God's presence and provision – the kind words spoken to you and the touches of his grace and mercy. These are his table in the presence of your enemies.

Being anointed | 12

> *You anoint my head with oil; my cup overflows.*
>
> **Psalm 23.5**

One of the great truths we can so easily forget is that we are marked with the presence of the Holy Spirit. We have been touched by him and so we are living temples that house the presence of God.

This is a beautiful truth with which to begin a time of prayer. It brings us back to the wonder of the relationship we have with God, but it is also a powerful truth to focus on in times of difficulty.

Wherever we go – whether we walk in times of peace and have an awareness of God's presence, or walk in gloom and confusion – we carry that anointing, that touch that will not be lifted from us. The one does not negate the other, but they exist together. We carry God's presence and anointing into the times of difficulty we face, and because of that we have a resource that is greater than anything else.

What brings us comfort and joy is to know that awareness of his presence. It is for this reason that it is so helpful to spend some time every day recalling Jesus' presence with us, either by spending a few minutes saying the name 'Jesus', or by recalling the beautiful verse, 'I bear your name, LORD God Almighty' (Jeremiah 15.16). Recalling these words in times of quiet arms us with the truth, which we can then take into times of turmoil.

Pursued by goodness | 13

There is something wonderful about knowing that goodness and love follow us every day whether we sense it or not. Some days we may be very open to the truth that goodness and love follow us, while on other days they may seem to be totally absent! Yet David proclaims their presence every single day.

If goodness and love are there every day, we do not have to ask God to give them to us. How can he if he has already done so? What we can ask for is that he opens our eyes to see where his goodness and love may be for us at any given time.

We are far too used to assuming that the things of God are not there because we cannot feel them. Perhaps they are and have been with us all the time, but we can't feel them because we are not tuned into them.

Jesus promised he would be with us always; he is goodness and love personified. This prayer is simple to pray, but can be quite transforming: ask Jesus where he is right now. Is he within you, beside you or around you? There is no correct answer – he has been following you, and probably leading you all day long. Find his presence and enjoy it.

You'll never walk alone! | 14

This is both a statement of reality and a statement of intent. As Jesus is always with us, and because our bodies are temples of the Holy Spirit, we cannot get away from his presence. That is the sentiment behind Psalm 139.7, 'Where can I go from your Spirit?' The answer is nowhere!

However, there is something important about David deciding to 'dwell in the house of the LORD'. In other words, he chose to dwell in that place. We make a similar decision when we choose to heed the words of Jesus when he says, "Remain in my love." (John 15.9)

Jesus has revealed his on-going presence with us and it is a matter of choice as to whether we take that seriously – but the good news is that we can make that choice. We have the permission and the authority to make the choice that we will live in the knowledge of his continual presence with us, whatever our feelings might tell us.

If we do make that choice, then every prayer we pray will be uttered face to face with Jesus; every dark moment will be faced in the company of the light of the world, and every lonely hour will be shared with the one who said he would be with us always.

Loving people is loving God

> *God...will not forget your work and the love you have shown him as you have helped his people and continue to help them.*
>
> **Hebrews 6.10**

The beauty of this verse is that it puts so much of our work and effort into context: anything we do to help another person is actually a gift of love to God, and he does not forget that.

So often we can be surrounded by the enormous needs of the world. We may give some money or time for a cause, but ultimately a little voice within us asks if it is really worth it? The need is so great and our contribution so small. Closer to home, if we offer a helping hand to someone perhaps they may not seem to appreciate it or even notice what we have done. Again, it is tempting to ask: was it worth it?

This verse shouts out at us, "Yes, it really is worth it." The reason is because what we are doing is not just about the immediate help that we give, but about what else our giving achieves. It is an act of love to God as well, a blessing to God that he remembers.

As you carry on caring in whatever way you can, and whatever you give, catch this vision: it is "For you, Father."

Be strong in grace

> *You then, my son, be strong in the grace that is in Christ Jesus.*
>
> **2 Timothy 2.1**

Strength is usually something that we measure in terms of our own personal ability – how much weight we can lift or how far we can run. It would be tempting to think of strong Christians in similar terms, such as how many converts they make and how many people they witness to in a particular day. To be strong in grace, however, puts the idea of strength into a totally different context.

Grace is precisely what we cannot achieve by our own efforts. It is what God freely gives us because of his love for us. When we are commanded to be strong in grace, it is precisely the opposite of human strength; it is a deliberate turning away from our own efforts and a seeking to draw on another source of strength.

The Bible speaks about the effects of grace in different ways. It is by grace that we resist temptation (Titus 2.12) and by grace that we receive help and mercy when we need it (Hebrews 4.16).

As followers of the God of grace, our calling is not so much to wonder what can be achieved today by our own efforts, but instead to draw on the amazing resources of heaven and then really see what can be achieved. As you look to the day ahead, what is it you cannot do in your own strength? Hold this before God, and seek the strength of his grace for it.

> *Be joyful always...*
> *for this is God's*
> *will for you in*
> *Christ Jesus.*
>
> **1 Thessalonians 5.16–18**

Being joyful | 1

It is natural for Christians to want to do God's will, and walking outside his will may be a terrifying thought. The trouble is that we can be crippled into inaction because we are so frightened of getting it wrong.

Over these next three days, we will be looking at three actions we can take which we are told are what God wants for us. It is actually very releasing to think that God is far more concerned about the attitude of our hearts than the particular details of what we do in our lives.

The first calling is to be joyful always. This is not easy, but it does begin to be a possibility when we capture the truth that joy is not the same as present momentary happiness. We may well be in situations that do not make us happy, and indeed may actually make us miserable, but even in those situations we can have joy.

Joy brings a different perspective to life. Happiness is most often judged by the present moment, while joy brings a Christian understanding of hope into the situation. Hope is believing God has more for us than what we are currently experiencing, and this is what brings joy to us.

Take stock of the situations in your life which are far from 'happy'. In each of these situations Jesus is there with his presence and his power.

Being prayerful | 2

> '...pray continually...
> for this is God's
> will for you in
> Christ Jesus.'
>
> **1 Thessalonians 5.17–18**

The idea of praying for even a relatively short period of time can fill some people with a sense of bewilderment, so it may feel daunting to read that God wants us to pray continually! As we are nowhere near that, how can we ever please God?

If we take prayer in the conventionally understood sense, of setting aside a period of time to talk to God, and we were to do that continually, we would never get anything else done. Presumably Paul is talking about something different here.

Prayer is actually the outworking of our belief that there is a God who loves us and cares for us. It is about seeking to be attentive to him as much as we can throughout the day, and reacting to situations not simply from our own attitudes, but by seeking to catch his attitude to situations. One way you can seek to do this is to let the word 'Jesus' be part of your breathing. As you say his name, you will find yourself catching his heart.

Someone once said that to pray everywhere all the time probably means that you have to start somewhere some of the time! So start small: spend the next five minutes doing nothing but letting the name 'Jesus' run through your mind to bring you into his presence.

> '...give thanks in all circumstances, for this is God's will for you in Christ Jesus.'
>
> **1 Thessalonians 5.18**

Being thankful | 3

Sometimes it is easy and natural to give thanks; at other times, especially when we are surrounded by trying circumstances or if we feel that God has let us down, we may wonder what to give thanks for, and why.

It would, of course, be true to say that there is always something for which we can give thanks. The very fact that we are in a living relationship with God is something that is entirely his initiative, and is something for which we can be thankful. But actually it is more than that. It is about our attitude and our focus. If we can give thanks in difficult circumstances, it says something about us. We are not focused simply on our own needs or the enormity of our problems when we turn to face him.

For what do we give thanks in these situations? It probably doesn't matter; what we are doing is seeking to develop an attitude focused on God in all circumstances.

Whatever your situation, take a moment now to turn to him and give thanks. It doesn't matter what you give thanks for, simply turn to face our generous God.

How do I find healing?

What do we have to do to get healed? It is a serious question. Many people read the accounts of Jesus healing the sick and hear about the healing ministry in church and ask, could it happen to me, and more importantly, how?

> 'For I desire mercy, not sacrifice, and acknowledgment of God rather than burnt offerings.'
>
> **Hosea 6.6 (NIV)**
>
> 'I want you to know GOD, not go to more prayer meetings.'
>
> **(The Message)**

This question of 'how' has led people to chase healing. They pursue speakers who are reputed to have great gifts of healing, or make bargains with God about what they will do if he heals them. However, if it was that simple and we were guaranteed healing after jumping through certain hoops, the queue would be enormous!

In this verse, the prophet Hosea brings us back to one fundamental principle that in itself does not guarantee healing, but certainly brings us to the very heart of God. We must seek a relationship with God before we seek healing. Why? Healing may well flow when we discover the joy of knowing God, but we will also gain so much more. We gain the peace of his presence, the joy of knowing that he is there at all times and the pleasure of hearing his voice as we speak to him in prayer.

Before you ask God for anything particular today, spend time finding his presence, not for what you might get out of it but simply because he enjoys being with you.

> *Each one should use whatever gift he has received to serve others, faithfully administering God's grace in its various forms.*
> **1 Peter 4.10**

Passing on grace

The implication of this verse is that we have been entrusted with a reservoir of God's grace and we have a choice whether or not to open it. Of course, it is God's wish that we let grace flow at all times, but we are his co-workers in this process. The alternative, of course, is that we open other reservoirs that may be present within us – perhaps of anger or bitterness, or even reservoirs that we may think have dried up, but which can have a negative effect on others.

However, this passage is addressed to 'each one', to all of us. If you are coming into contact with other people today, which reservoir will you open up for them?

God has shown remarkable grace to each of us; he gave us Jesus to demonstrate his kindness to us. It is worth considering how much grace you are really showing towards yourself. If you can begin to see yourself through God's eyes, you are more likely to see others through his graceful eyes as well.

What does it mean to you to be loved by God? Take it seriously and enjoy it.

The reign of God | 1

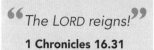

To say that the Lord reigns is to acknowledge that everything that goes on in this world and in our lives is happening within God's arena. It does not mean that he has caused everything, or that he approves of all that happens under his reign, but it does change everything.

One implication of the reign of God is that he has an opinion about what happens on earth. Many times, for example, Jesus spoke about justice: Matthew 12.18-21 quotes Isaiah's vision that links the ministry of the Messiah to the bringing about of justice; and at the beginning of Luke 18 the parable about persistence speaks of God wanting to bring about justice on earth. There are many things happening in this world, or to us, that Jesus sees as unjust. His mission was to bring about justice, and these things bother him; he is concerned about the injustice of them.

It is a wonderful thing to sit before the Lord and bring to him the particular circumstances of the world that concern us, or bring to him the circumstances of our lives that weigh us down, and to seek his view about them. What does he think of these events? As you ponder these things before God, perhaps there are emotions stirring within you that are actually his emotions. Begin to feel his heart.

> **"***The LORD reigns!***"**
> **1 Chronicles 16.31**

Another aspect of the kingship of God is that he is an active king. He is not powerless; rather, he is a God who acts, who responds to the cries of his people. However, on many occasions he doesn't seem to be a God who sees injustice and sovereignly intervenes. Instead, he often seems to operate through us.

Hebrews 4.16 talks about us approaching the 'throne of grace' so that we might receive help. In other words, God's throne is not distant and unapproachable, but is something to which we can come and from which transforming power flows.

God does indeed reign – he has a mission to change the injustice under which so many live – but it is us who are so often the doorways through which that mission flows. It begins with our prayer, our coming to him, approaching the throne of grace to find the help that is needed. It may well be that we are the answer to the injustice that grips many; we may be the hands of God to bring healing to others, a voice to the downtrodden, or action for those who cannot act for themselves.

Whatever the solution to an injustice, it begins with our coming to God's throne of grace, compassion and power so that what is needed may flow from that.

The beginning of prayer

'Therefore, brothers and sisters, since we have confidence to enter the Most Holy Place by the blood of Jesus...'

Hebrews 10.19

This verse, which is about the way we approach God, says something very powerful. It tells us that prayer doesn't begin with us. It begins with the fact that Jesus died for us – something he did without asking us what we thought about it and something that happened before we were born. We now live after that event and nothing can change the truth that it happened.

The effect of that action was to open the door for us to enter the presence of God: before all of us stands an open door through which we have every right to enter, a door through which we are beckoned and welcomed. This door leads to a place of amazing power. Beyond the door is the 'Most Holy Place', the throne room of God and the place of his presence. All that is needed is for us to have the confidence to go into that room and know that we are accepted in that place.

This is what makes such a difference to our prayers. It is not us speaking words into the air, but actually voicing our needs and concerns in the very throne room of God. When we grasp that, our prayers can change. This is where you are right now, so speak to him.

> *May the God of peace, who through the blood of the eternal covenant brought back from the dead our Lord Jesus, that great Shepherd of the sheep, equip you with everything good for doing his will...*
>
> **Hebrews 13.20–21**

God could use me if . . .

As we look ahead to what the next 24 hours hold for us, a good prayer to pray is that God would use us. The trouble is we often feel that God could use us more if…

It may be that we feel he could use us if we were more gifted, or if we had more time or more overt opportunities to be used. This verse brings us back to a profound truth. It begins by speaking about what God has already done. It goes on to talk about what else he can do for us by equipping us.

In other words, any sense of our being equipped today is because God has already poured out his energy and power by raising Jesus from the dead. He did that because of 'the eternal covenant'. In other words, it was something he promised to do; it was unthinkable that he would not do it. By the same token, it is unthinkable that God will not equip you for all he has called you to today.

As you look toward the hours ahead and all that you will do, you are equipped for his work. He would no more send you out without his presence than he would leave Jesus in the tomb. Let this truth be within you: 'I can do everything through him who gives me strength.' Say these words, and let the truth of them touch you.

Worshipping the Father

>"Yet a time is coming and has now come when the true worshippers will worship the Father in spirit and truth, for they are the kind of worshippers the Father seeks."
>
> **John 4.23**

Let's look at just six words from this statement by Jesus: 'true worshippers will worship the Father'. These few succinct words prompt the great question, who do you worship?

Such a question can make us feel guilty, especially if our reaction to the word 'father' is unhelpful or distant. However, far from trying to make us feel guilty, Jesus is actually offering a stunning invitation. Those six words are preceded by the phrase, 'a time is coming and has now come'. The time is about him; it is his coming that changes everything about worship, because Jesus is the perfect picture of what God the Father is really like. To have seen Jesus, to have tasted his compassion and to have been touched by his forgiveness and grace, is to have received the touch of our Father God.

Jesus reveals the wonder of God's fatherhood no matter what your experience of earthly fatherhood may be. Your joy is to explore that wonder, to be touched by it and to say 'yes' to the truth that the Father has turned himself towards you and his love for you is real. This is the beginning of true worship. Let the word 'Father' roll through your mind with a sense of worship, tenderness and longing in your heart.

The kingdom is within me | 1

" ...the kingdom of God is within you. **"**
Luke 17.21

This statement by Jesus can be translated in two ways. Some translations state that the kingdom of God is 'among you', or 'in your midst', and others phrase it, 'within you'. Perhaps these translations are not so different.

Jesus originally said these words to the Pharisees, who were looking for signs of the coming of the kingdom. Jesus encouraged them not to look for signs of the kingdom elsewhere, but rather to be aware of the presence of the kingdom in their midst – and what was in their very midst was himself. If they could but see it, the fullness of the kingdom of God would be so close to them; they could probably even feel his breath on them.

Although we don't have the physical presence of Jesus with us as the Pharisees did, he does live in us through the Holy Spirit, and for that reason we, too, can proclaim that the kingdom is within us. All the resources of what God's kingdom has to bring are actually as close as the air within our lungs. To have the Spirit dwelling in us is to have every fruit and every gift so close to us.

Wherever you may be right now, pause to proclaim, "The kingdom of God is within me."

The kingdom is within all of us | 2

" ...the kingdom of God is within you. "

Luke 17.21

All too often we compare ourselves to others, and either feel completely second class or end up looking for their hidden faults to try to bring them down to our level. When we start to go down this road of comparison we rob ourselves, for what we are neglecting is the truth that every single one of us carries the wonder of the presence of the kingdom of God within us. We also rob God because he is denied the pleasure of seeing his kingdom within us acknowledged and flourishing.

When we begin to compare ourselves to others, we are looking at the wrong thing, at the outward shell of the temple, whereas we should be looking at what the temple bears – namely, the wonder of the kingdom enshrined in the presence of the Holy Spirit.

The Spirit who is within me is exactly the same Spirit who dwells in every Christian I admire; it is the same Spirit who dwelt in Jesus. God gives the same Spirit to us all. What perhaps makes the difference is our willingness to yield to the Spirit – but he is always there, present within us, loving us and waiting to live through us.

Ponder this as you compare yourself to others: the same Spirit who lived in Jesus lives in you.

> *Come to the sanctuary, which he has consecrated for ever.*
>
> **2 Chronicles 30.8**

Finding sanctuary

There is something very beautiful about this invitation from King Hezekiah to his people, who had wandered away from God. What he is saying is that wherever they might feel they are spiritually, there was a place that they can always return to – a place of sanctuary and rest where they could meet with God. This is the place that God himself has established, a place that speaks about his willingness and desire that we come back to him.

The joyful thing is that this sanctuary is not far from us; in fact, it is within us. Paul speaks about us being temples of the Holy Spirit and the Spirit's presence within us is the sanctuary that he has set apart.

What this means is that the God we long for is never far from us. In fact, he is only as far away as it takes to say the word, 'Jesus'. To speak that name purposefully to Jesus is to speak face to face with the one who gave up everything to reveal the Father's love to us. Speaking his name is about coming back to the sanctuary and finding rest. Take a few minutes to do that now.

Healing is Jesus doing good

> *Then Jesus said to them, "I ask you, which is lawful on the Sabbath: to do good or to do evil, to save life or to destroy it?"*
>
> **Luke 6.9**

What is interesting about this statement is that it is set within the context of a story about healing. While Jesus was in a synagogue on the Sabbath, he came across a man there who had a physical need. We are also told of the presence of religious leaders who were watching intently to see what Jesus would do on this holy day. To their indignation, and presumably to the sick man's delight, Jesus healed him. Then he went on to talk about why he healed. He actually puts it so simply: that healing is about doing good, and is the opposite of doing evil.

We may find ourselves in a position of need, and that need might be for healing. Invariably, we are faced with the question, does God want to heal me? These words of Jesus are so simple and powerful – of course he does! If we have any doubt about it, let's ask ourselves this question in the way that Jesus put it: does he want to do good to me or to do evil?

We have made healing so complicated. When we look at the ministry of Jesus as he saw it, it becomes something much simpler. Healing is about Jesus doing good, so bring your needs to him with confidence.

Carrying his presence

> *Then the temple of the LORD was filled with a cloud, and the priests could not perform their service because of the cloud, for the glory of the LORD filled the temple of God.*
>
> **2 Chronicles 5.13–14**

The picture these words convey is quite dramatic. At the service of consecration, the priests, who no doubt had their own expectations of what was meant to happen in the service, were utterly bowled over by the sense of the presence of God and they were unable to do what they expected to do. No doubt their sense of the presence of God changed, and eventually they would not sense his presence as they had on that occasion, but I imagine that they took their duties even more seriously, knowing that God was in their midst.

We don't have clouds floating around us to remind us of his presence, but we have something equally as powerful. Paul writes of us: 'The Spirit of him who raised Jesus from the dead is living in you.' We have existing within us something that is similar to the presence of God that dwelt in that temple. While the priests could feel and see that presence we have to take it by faith, but it is still as real.

Whatever we face today, let us go into each situation aware that the Spirit of him who raised Jesus from the dead is living in us.

A new adventure

> *Remember Jesus Christ, raised from the dead, descended from David. This is my gospel, for which I am suffering even to the point of being chained like a criminal. But God's word is not chained.*
>
> **2 Timothy 2.8–9**

To think of something being unchained is to think of it as wild, unpredictable and free to do as it wants. That is how God wants his word to be with us. The trouble is that many people do chain up the word of God and do not give it the freedom to touch their lives. It is not so much that we should read the Bible, but that the Bible should be allowed to read us.

A systematic plan for reading the Bible ensures that we do not simply keep going to the passages that comfort us. Comfort is good, but growth is better.

As you read a Bible passage, ask yourself, what does this passage say about God? What would strike you if you were reading this for the first time? What is there within this passage that particularly challenges or encourages you? Is there anything here that the Holy Spirit wants to underline for you? What verse or phrase can you write down to take into the day ahead?

As you engage with the Bible in this way, you can begin to loosen the chains around it and enter into a daily adventure with God through his word.

> *Abraham reasoned that God could raise the dead.*

Hebrews 11.19

Where is Jesus for you?

In his letter to the Hebrews, the author examines some of the 'heroes' of the Old Testament to highlight the importance of faith. As he does, we discover snippets about the meaning of faith.

One of those he lifts up is Abraham and the story of Abraham being asked to sacrifice the son who holds so many promises for him. What we learn from this verse is that Abraham's faith was not based simply on a blind obedience to what God had spoken, but rather that he took time to ponder the command and seek a vision of how the future would work. Perhaps he even had a vision of himself and his son walking back down the mountain. Abraham knew that he had to obey God, but what he also had was a vision of how he was going to do it.

Like Abraham, we are all called to trust God in some way. It may be that our future looks bleak, it may be that we feel an insecurity about our lives, it may be that we are burdened with what we have to get through. It is hard to suddenly be different, or relaxed and happy, when deep down we are not. But what we can do is to start by finding a vision for our day. This can begin by simply asking Jesus where he is for you on this day. Ask him this question and see what image or thought comes to mind. Hold that image in your mind and let that feed your faith for what God can do in you today.

Recapturing the dream

'So God created man in his own image...'

Genesis 1.27

There have been many discussions about what it means to be created in the image of God, but what it certainly conveys is that there is something wonderful about us – we contain something of the presence of God within us. Of course, God's original plans were marred as the human race turned away from him to walk in its own way, but Jesus came to change that.

Jesus came as the image of the invisible God in human form, supremely bearing and reflecting the image of God (perhaps in a way that was meant to be true of all of us). It is as we find the joy of the presence of Jesus within us that we recapture the reality of what it means to bear the image of God.

The implications of this are profound: we bear God's presence. As we go about our daily business (even without thinking about it), there is not a person we meet who will not come into contact with God – simply because we bear his presence. Since these people meet with us, they will be meeting God within us. This truth opens up the way for us to quietly pray in as many situations as we can, "Jesus, what do you want to do here?" Panic may grip us that he wants us to preach a full-blown sermon on the bus or train, but if we tune our ear to him, his promptings will be more likely to be to perform small acts of kindness and offer words of encouragement to those with whom we come into contact. You bear Jesus' presence and image this very day, so be bold enough to take this seriously.

What is Jesus praying today?

> *Therefore he is able to save completely those who come to God through him, because he always lives to intercede for them.*
>
> **Hebrews 7.25**

There are times when prayer seems to flow and other times when it's like talking to a brick wall! This is probably the experience of most people.

Whatever our particular struggle with prayer at the moment, this staggering fact sheds a new light on everything: Jesus is praying for us. Whether we are praying or not, he is; whether prayer seems exciting or turgid to us, the most intimate conversation between Jesus and the Father is going on and we are the subject of that conversation. But what is Jesus praying for?

Jesus is both enthroned in heaven and dwelling in us through his Holy Spirit. Our bodies house his presence. Can we therefore catch the whisper of his intercession?

It is as simple as this: begin by dwelling on the Father's love for you and ask Jesus what his intercession is for you today. The answer may come in a variety of ways – thoughts, words, pictures, Bible verses – but pay attention to whatever comes spontaneously into your mind as you ask that question. Write it down and ponder it as his prayer for you today.

Spiritual battles

'Resist him, standing firm in the faith...'

1 Peter 5.9

The very mention of a topic such as spiritual warfare can be alarming for many people, raising all manner of images and questions. Indeed, the image that Peter uses in the preceding verse is of the devil as a roaring lion, so that does little to bring comfort to us. It seems to add a whole new dimension to our spiritual lives in which we would probably rather not get involved!

The good news about this verse is that actually we are not asked to do any more than we are already seeking to do – and the results are staggering. Peter calls us to stand firm in our faith; in other words, to hold fast to what we believe to be true about God and us.

Perhaps the main arena for the spiritual battle in which we find ourselves is that of our position with God. The work of the enemy is to condemn, separating us from the knowledge of God's love for us. It is not so much that God should pour out any more love upon us – he has already given us Jesus – but the battle is about our ability to stand in the truth of what has already been revealed to us. Standing firm does not mean we have to reach out and grasp new things, but rather that we stand in the timeless truths of God's love for us personally. Specifically, this means God's self-giving in the person of Jesus and his dwelling in us and working through us in the person of the Holy Spirit.

Rejoice in the truth of these things for you and make them the focus of your own prayers of thanksgiving.

> **"** *Come to me, all you who are weary and burdened...* **"**
>
> **Matthew 11.28**

There's nothing you have to do first | 1

This beautiful invitation from Jesus cuts through a lot of thinking about us coming to him. Something inside often prevents us from coming to Jesus until we actively do something: perhaps we feel we can't come until we repent or have forgiven everyone, or until we have lived a good life. However, Jesus' invitation is quite the opposite: when we are weary, when we are burdened, when we feel the weight of sin upon us and when we don't know what to do next – these are exactly the moments to come him. All the things we need – rest, forgiveness and guidance – come from Jesus, but not until we approach him first.

So how do we come to Jesus? Coming to him begins with knowing that we can, that we are welcome in his presence whoever we are and whatever we have done. The main reason that most of us feel excluded from Jesus' presence is not because he is doing the excluding, but because we do it ourselves.

Jesus stands and makes this invitation today to everyone who is weary and burdened. It is an invitation to you. However distant you feel from him, speak his name with tenderness and meaning. He is waiting for you.

It's OK to be in need | 2

It has been said that one of the hardest things to do is to pray. We would much rather try to solve a problem ourselves, or even worry about it, than actually to bring the issue to Jesus and leave it at his feet.

There may be a number of reasons why we find praying such a hard thing to do. Part of it may be that to pray is to acknowledge that we need help and we are not self-sufficient – and that can be such a difficult thing for us to admit. Yet that is precisely what Jesus invites us to do with these words.

It is very noticeable in the Gospels that Jesus seemed to place a high value on people sharing their needs. It was often those who actually stepped out of the crowds or who came to him who received healing. We may think that seems quite odd. Surely he could see the needs of those around him? If he loved them so much why didn't he just get on with it and heal them?

We often have the idea that praying for our own needs should come at the end of the list of things we do in prayer: a time of worship, then thanksgiving, followed by a healthy dose of confession and then finally we can bring our requests to him. Actually, intercession for our needs is worship – it is acknowledging that he is the Lord and we have no power to help ourselves, and that we submit to his intervention in our lives. It really is OK to pray for your own needs!

> **"** ...all you who are weary and burdened... **"**
> **Matthew 11.28**

Don't go away! | 3

Part of the reason why it is difficult for us to admit a need is that it can be seen as a sign of weakness. If we are really spiritual, if God is really with us, then we feel we should never be sick or lack anything in our lives. Certainly we like to come across that way.

However, Jesus never condemned those who had needs. He had profound compassion on each of them and it was those people who admitted their needs to him who had the most stunning experiences of his love and grace. They experienced his touch, and his powerful grace flowed through them.

If we sense that we are in need, the wonderful news is that Jesus says, "Come" and not, "Go away." We can be so quick to tell ourselves that he is not interested in us or that there are others whose needs are much greater than ours, but Jesus says to everyone who sees themselves as laden or burdened, "Come."

Take a moment to assure yourself of the truth that God loves you so much he gave Jesus for you, then spend a few minutes in his presence and share your needs with him. He cares about you because you matter to him.

The promise of rest | 4

" ...and I will give you rest. "

Matthew 11.28

After Jesus' invitation that the weary and burdened should come to him, he gave them the promise of rest. Can we trust this promise? Could it be that Jesus may decide after all not to give us rest on this particular occasion? Jesus confidently makes this promise, not just as a promise to be there, looking out for us, but also because of what he went on to do: he died for us.

The rest that Jesus promises could be summed up in another place in the Gospels as living life 'to the full' (John 10.10). Jesus said that he came that we would have such a life. It is interesting to see that in the very next verse Jesus spoke of himself as the good shepherd who laid down his life for his sheep. In other words, the promise of abundant life for us is linked to the laying down of Jesus' life for us.

This is why we can be confident about this promise of rest, not because it is a promise of what Jesus will do, but because it is a declaration of what he has done. In dying for us, Jesus has opened up the way for us to enter the very presence of God, and our rest flows from being with him.

So it isn't a matter of Jesus continuing to ponder on whether or not to give us rest; he took that decision when he died for us. Rest is ours, if only we will come to him. Take a moment to consider the implications of this truth: Jesus laid down his life to give you abundant life.

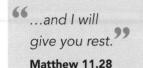

The river of rest | 5

Yesterday we looked at Jesus' promise to give us rest as something that is based on what he has already done for us. Let's look a little more at the nature of this gift.

The gift of rest is not a one-off experience for us, but rather a constant source of his working in our lives. Although many people can look back to singular experiences of the wonder of God's love when they felt his presence in a special way, or a touch of his grace and love, God's rest, peace and grace are not meant to be one-off experiences to which we can put a date in our diaries. Rather, they flow from God in a constant stream to us; the invitation God gives to the weary and burdened is not a single voucher that can only be used once. Jesus would be delighted if we sought his rest every single hour of every single day.

God may have blessed you in the past, but will you go back to him today? God may have assured you of his love for you in days gone by, what if he is seeking to do it again now?

Take a moment to let him give you a fresh sense of his love and touch today. He is waiting, and all you have to do is come to him and ask.

It's all about Jesus | 6

> **66** ...and I will give you rest. **99**
> **Matthew 11.28**

We have looked at the promise of rest and the continuing availability of that rest for us. The source of it is Jesus, but so often we seek a variety of other means to find the rest that only comes from him.

Actually, one of the loveliest aspects of this truth is that Jesus will be there for all of us. This is not an invitation to a specific group of holy people who have achieved the ability to leave their problems behind. It is precisely to the weary and the burdened that Jesus promises his active presence.

There may well be ways in which we can help ourselves find his presence, but the fact that he doesn't give any specific instructions means that it can't be too difficult. The first thing we need to remember is that Jesus is there to help. When we are preoccupied and struggling, the promise is that Jesus is there with help for us. Perhaps all it takes is to say his name, "Jesus." To speak his name is to recognise our need, to acknowledge his presence and to invite him into our situation.

Who you are does not matter, nor does it matter how good you have been. What matters is that you call on him and wait to see what happens.

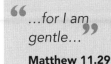

The gentleness of Jesus | 7

These simple words form the basis of our trust in coming to Jesus; when we come, we will not be turned away, nor will Jesus ridicule our needs. Rather, he will treat us with the gentleness for which our hearts yearn. This gentleness is not an act on his part, but rather it flows from the truth that he is gentle – which is his nature – so when we come to him, we come before the personification of gentleness.

This gentleness should inspire us to honesty. We do not have to hide anything away from Jesus nor be fearful that he will view us harshly. The reality is that he knows everything about us and is longing for us to bring all of ourselves to him. Nothing we share with him can shock him or change his attitude towards us.

Jesus' gentleness should also inspire us to emulate him. We are disciples of the one who said that he was gentle, and that is how we should also be. This attitude should define our dealings with others. How wonderful it would be if we were known for our gentleness by those who come into contact with us. Come now to Jesus and let his gentleness flow though you today.

What's the catch? | 8

66 ...and my burden is light. 99

Matthew 11.30

This phrase is quite a statement. It actually stands as a measuring line for the nature of our Christian lives. Is our faith a joy or is it a burden?

It is so easy to slip into the legalistic nature of religion: we ought to pray for a certain length of time each day, read so much of the Bible, give a proportion of our money and so on. Worse is when we do not meet the expectations that we or others have put upon ourselves, and then we feel guilty and discover that the faith that was meant to bring us freedom is actually a heavy burden that is a struggle for us.

Jesus said that it was never meant to be like this: his yoke should be easy and his burden is meant to be light. What is going wrong?

Legalism usually steps in to fill the void left by the lack of relationship. A good question to ask yourself when you are feeling burdened by your faith is, "Why am I doing it?" If you ask yourself why you read your Bible and the honest answer is because you are trying to get through a Bible plan, it is likely that legalism has crept in over your relationship with God. Similarly, if your prayers are more about simply saying words than speaking with God, again, you may want to rethink your motives.

The good news is that change can be immediate! If legalism has crept into your faith, begin to speak the word, "Jesus" as if he is right in front of you. Lay aside the ritual of religion and find the wonder of your relationship with him again.

> *But the people were thirsty for water there, and they grumbled against Moses.*
>
> **Exodus 17.3**

It's so easy to grumble

Time and time again we read of the Israelites wandering in the desert grumbling about their lot, and comparing what they had with some idealised memory of the past in which they conveniently forgot the harder parts.

If we are honest, we can probably identify with their grumbling, as this is something we all tend to indulge in many times throughout the day.

Grumbling often begins when we start to look at what we do not have, rather than what we do have. When that happens, rather than dwelling on what we have in abundance we tend to focus on what we lack, which can easily lead on to apportioning blame for our lack and judging others. This is exactly what the Israelites did – they took their eyes off their freedom, off their vision of God and off the divine provision given to them on a daily basis and recalled a rosy past, forgetting the slavery, beatings and helplessness of their previous situation.

We may not be wandering in a desert and have never been slaves, but what we do have in common with the Israelites is our propensity to grumble, to take our eyes off what we have and fix them on what we do not. Take a moment to pause, thank God for something you do have as you touch each finger of both hands; keep going if you want to, even after your fingers have run out! God always wants us to come to him with our needs, but by beginning to give thanks our awareness of his goodness to us will increase.

Sticking close to God

'Suddenly there was such a violent earthquake that the foundations of the prison were shaken. At once all the prison doors flew open, and everybody's chains came loose.'

Acts 16.26

Paul and Silas were in prison worshipping God and presumably enjoying fellowship with him when there was an almighty earthquake. The doors to the prison flew open and the prisoners' chains fell from their bodies.

Put yourself in that situation. Imagine feeling that you had been unfairly imprisoned and something suddenly happened that caused the doors to open and your chains to come loose. What would you do? I imagine that most of us would praise God for his deliverance and run, but not Paul and Silas! What they never seemed to forget was that their relationship with God took precedence over their physical circumstances.

In their difficult situation we find them connecting with God, whom they trusted. When the situation changed dramatically, they made no assumptions about what God was doing, but stayed connected to him. Presumably they felt his restraining hand encouraging them to stay where they were. It is a sad fact that many people are closer to God in times of desperation, but when the situation changes they are not so quick to pray and seek the God who loves them. Whether life is good or bad, whether you are in a time of seeming captivity or freedom, come back to your Father who longs for fellowship with you, whatever you might be feeling.

'They drew back and fell to the ground.'

John 18.6

Physical reactions

Physical manifestations of a religious experience are fascinating phenomena. Some people testify with a genuine heart about significant moments when their bodies have physically manifested something of the presence of God. It may be falling over, shaking, laughing, crying, exuberant praise or a variety of other actions. What this particular verse highlights to us is that there can be a marked difference between what is going on with our bodies and what is going on in our hearts.

The soldiers who came to arrest Jesus certainly had an experience of the presence of God – he was standing right in front of them. Their bodies reacted to his presence as they fell down without any prompting. What did not seem to happen was any spiritual transformation within their hearts.

This is not in any way making a judgment about physical manifestations – they may happen or they may not. However, whenever we sense our bodies reacting to the presence of God, it may be wise to pray that our hearts will be equally touched by him.

If we sense the presence of God in any way, let it be a signpost to us that God is nudging us, and let us be quick to open our hearts to him as well. And if we feel nothing at all, the truth still stands that God loves us with an unending love and that he is present with us in every part of our lives. Whatever you might be feeling right now, sit with him and enjoy being in his company.

Catching God's answers

But Naaman went away angry and said, "I thought that he would surely come out to me and stand and call on the name of the LORD his God, wave his hand over the spot and cure me of my leprosy."

2 Kings 5.11

Praying for healing is a beautiful ministry, and is being developed in many churches today. However, it is not without its problems, one of which is our expectations as we seek healing. We often come to Jesus with quite fixed ideas about how he will answer our prayers. If he answers us in a way that differs from our own expectations, we are likely to miss the opportunity of recognising him at work.

This was Naaman's problem: he had a pretty clear idea of how he thought God would bring healing to him, and we are told that he went into a rage when it was suggested that God might do it differently (2 Kings 5.12).

Psalm 5.3 encourages us to lay our requests before God and 'wait in expectation'. The calling on us is to be open to the many ways in which our creative God brings his answers to us. If we are only looking in one particular direction, we may well miss him altogether.

Take a moment to do just this. Lay out your requests before God, thank him that each of them has been heard, and wait in expectation for what he will do.

Being part of God's healing plan

' ... and his flesh was restored and became clean like that of a young boy.'

2 Kings 5.14

Does God use you? The problem that many of us find when considering this question is that we tend to compare ourselves to others before answering. Yes, he may well use us, but not as much as other people.

Perhaps God doesn't view this issue in the same way that we do; every one of us is equally important to his purposes. The story of Naaman's healing is amazing in many ways. One of its key features is this question: who was responsible for his healing? As you read this story, you will discover that there were numerous people directly involved, and every one played a key part in helping this man be healed: the slave to Naaman's wife, the King of Aram, the King of Israel, Elisha, Naaman's servants and attendants – even a river! At any point, one of these people could have been a block to the whole process and the outcome might have been different.

You may not think you have a ministry that is 'up-front' or glamorous, but every ministry, no matter how small it seems to be, is a massive part of God's plan. You have the opportunity to be a faithful participant in his dreams for this world. It may only be a kind word or an encouraging smile, but these touches may be incredibly significant to someone, even though you may not regard them as dramatic or life changing. What may seem a small act to you will be viewed quite differently by them and by God.

Finding God's approval

It is probably true that we all seek the praise or approval of others. We want to be liked and we want to know that we are appreciated for what we do. The danger is that we can become caught up in a never-ending surge of activity to find other people's approval anew, and if we do not find it we can find ourselves in a pit of despair and self-doubt.

It is important to do good to others, but in this verse Jesus warns against us seeking to find our identity in the approval of others; his encouragement is for us to find our approval from God. What is startling about this statement is that it confirms that God already approves of us.

For some people, the constant quest to seek the approval of others is precisely because they are not certain of God's approval. Jesus bids us to stop thinking in that way and find his approval first, and then let our actions flow from that.

Take this verse and use it to seek to catch God's love, approval and desire for you: 'I belong to my lover, and his desire is for me' (Song of Songs 7.10). What more approval could you possibly want?

Futile thinking

So I tell you this, and insist on it in the Lord, that you must no longer live as the Gentiles do, in the futility of their thinking.

Ephesians 4.17

In this verse, Paul talks about living in the futility of our thinking. The context of this passage is that of immorality. We may be able to convince ourselves that a certain action or way of thinking is fine, but if it does not align to the truth revealed in the Bible, we run the risk of following the futility of our thinking as opposed to the revelation that God brings.

This is not just true within the context of immorality, it is also true in the way that we think about ourselves. The Bible reveals the awesome truth of the love of God – that he loves each one of us personally and intimately. Our thinking can often contradict that revelation. We may think that we are unloved and unlovable, and find ourselves dwelling on that and allowing it to take root in our hearts instead. This is the futility of our thinking, and it is at odds with what the Bible reveals. It comes down to a simple choice: which path are we going to follow and where are we going to allow our minds to take us?

You may think you are being humble in wondering if God could ever love you; Paul would probably call this futile thinking! Take a moment to bring your thinking into line with his. You are deeply loved by God who gave Jesus for you, and his presence will never leave you.

It's not just us who are loved!

'But we ought always to thank God for you, brothers loved by the Lord, because from the beginning God chose you to be saved through the sanctifying work of the Spirit and through belief in the truth.'

2 Thessalonians 2.13

Life would sometimes be a lot easier if it were not for people! You might have an inspiring time with God, finding great consolation in his love for you, and then go out to face the world. At that point life can very quickly take a turn for the worse. It's not just people 'out there' who seem intent on being difficult; sometimes it is those people closer to home who cause you problems, such as family members or other Christians.

The truth is that we are all chosen and loved by God. Today's verse brings us up short by reminding us of this. You are his dearly loved child, but so is everyone else, even those you find difficult.

Criticizing and judging others is a very easy route to take, so before entertaining unkind thoughts about anyone, it is a good practice to hold them in your mind and remind yourself that although you may find them difficult, they are loved by God to such an extent that Jesus chose to die for them.

It may be that even as you read these words, there is someone who comes to mind. Think about them and 'see' them as deeply loved by God.

'...seek his
face always.'

1 Chronicles 16.11

Finding God right now

This command to actively seek the presence of God at all times seems so challenging, yet what underlies it is very good news for us: God can be found at all times. If not, then why encourage us to seek him?

Seeking God becomes much easier if we know he is there. It is a hopeless task to search for someone who is absent, but to seek our God, who is always there, becomes a search full of excitement and possibility.

The practical application of this command to seek God is far-reaching: what is it you are lacking? Whether it is strength, confidence, wisdom, love or patience, the answer comes down to a simple command: to seek God's presence first.

How? There are probably countless ways, but it starts with the knowledge that God is there, waiting.

Ask yourself, "Where is Jesus for me right now?" As you engage with this question, be aware that it is Jesus showing you where he is for you at this particular moment, and not you trying to imagine where he might be. Find him, rejoice in his presence and enjoy him.

Let yourself be drawn back to God through the day by regularly repeating these words, "Seek his face always."

The Father is always at work

Jesus and the things he did were clearly linked to the work of his Father, but when Jesus explained this the people listening took such offence they tried to kill him. It is amazing that Jesus took such an incredible risk to say something potentially so dangerous. Presumably, the reason was that his statement contained something Jesus really wanted to be heard: that his Father was always at work, no matter what people were going through.

> 'Jesus said to them, "My Father is always at his work to this very day, and I, too, am working . . . the Son can do nothing by himself; he can do only what he sees his Father doing, because whatever the Father does the Son also does."'
>
> **John 5.17–19**

So what is God doing? Paul writes in Philippians 2.13 (NLT), 'For God is working in you, giving you the desire and the power to do what pleases him.' In other words, the Father is at work in you right now, doing what he can to draw you to him and to keep you close.

You may face struggles, and at times may wonder how you are going to get through them. The truth is that you will get through because the Father is at work in you, seeking to turn you more and more to him. Hold on to these words today: 'The Father is at work in me.'

It's already done | 1

There can sometimes be an element of 'will he won't he?', or 'you never know your luck!' in our prayers, and we may not be particularly surprised if some of our prayers seem to go unanswered. In fact, we probably think that God would never have answered them anyway!

Part of the reason for thinking like this is because we struggle to understand why God would want to do something extraordinary for us in the first place.

This phrase at the end of Psalm 22 encourages a different attitude to the activity of God. Here, God is presented as the deliverer who has already wrought our deliverance for us rather than someone who rarely does anything extraordinary nowadays. In 2 Corinthians 1.20, Paul makes more sense of this when he writes, 'For no matter how many promises God has made, they are "Yes" in Christ'. In other words, when Jesus lived, died and was raised again, he did all that was necessary for the promises of God to be fulfilled.

It is no longer worth questioning why God would do something special for you, but instead spend time looking at what he has already done for you and reflect on how this might alter your prayers.

It's already done | 2

> '...for he has done it.'
>
> **Psalm 22.31**

This glorious truth – that in Christ, God has already done everything needed for your prayers to be answered – deserves to be put into practice. A simple way to do this is to take time reflecting on what difference the life, death and resurrection of Jesus makes to the particular prayers you offer to God.

If you are praying for someone in need, the difference this truth makes is that God has already demonstrated the depth of his love for that person by giving them the most precious thing he has to give. Why would he hold anything else back?

A situation that may be causing you anxiety can be transformed by recognizing that Jesus has been raised to such an exalted position that everything else is under his feet and subject to him. Throughout his life, Jesus revealed God's true nature. If your prayer today is for yourself but you aren't sure how God might react, visualise yourself approaching the Jesus of the New Testament. Then approach God with a similar ease and joy. As you bring to God those things you want to lift to him, rather than simply supplying a list, ponder each of your requests from the perspective of what God has already done for you in that situation.

The wrong attitude when praying can so often prevent God's graceful response from being heard and received, yet he gave us Jesus so we might approach his throne with confidence. 'He has done it' is what should shape your prayers today.

> *But Moses sought the favour of the LORD his God.*

Exodus 32.11

Enjoy God's favour

After being in God's presence for 40 days, Moses came down the mountainside to discover that in his absence his people had started to worship an image of a golden calf. This angered God to such an extent that he planned to destroy them all. At this dramatic point, today's verse records that Moses sought the favour of the Lord.

It was not that God had ever removed his favour from Moses or that it was now hidden, but rather that Moses needed to come back to that place of intimacy that already existed between God and himself; from there he cried out to God and God heard. In a moment of real tension and crisis, Moses needed to focus on the truth and wonder of God once again.

In the same way, when you seek the favour and intimacy of God, it is not that he has disappeared, but rather that you may have moved away and are feeling distant. God's delight in you never changes, but your belief in it does. Come back to him every day and enjoy his favour. It may be that you want to come back to him right now and find his love afresh.

Your words

'Eli answered, "Go in peace, and may the God of Israel grant you what you have asked of him."'

1 Samuel 1.17

Eli, a priest, had been listening to Hannah crying out to God for a son. Initially he thought she was drunk, but on hearing the real reason for her heartfelt prayer he spoke these words. Hannah's prayer was answered and she did indeed bear a child, suggesting that Eli's words had carried authority and power.

Your words also have power and you need to take what you say seriously. Many people testify to the destructive nature of words spoken to them; sometimes even one negative sentence can have a lasting effect on the way people regard themselves. Refusing to pass on gossip, choosing not to criticize, trying to replace unkind words with a positive comment and looking people in the eyes and thanking them are all very practical ways of using your words as a blessing to the people you meet.

When you communicate with someone today, what will be the lasting effect of your communication?

> *'Yet the LORD longs to be gracious to you...'*
>
> **Isaiah 30.18**

The God of grace

Isaiah spoke these words to a people who had wandered away from God and turned their backs on him. Despite this, God wanted to communicate his longing and passionate love for them. They may indeed have turned their backs on him, but his desire was to be gracious.

How much more does God long to be gracious to us? Sometimes it is tempting to imagine that when he sees us approaching, an air of weariness strikes him, yet nothing could be further from the truth. God is gracious and he longs to show his grace to us in far greater measure than we have already experienced, because the extent of his grace is limitless.

We are all urged to extend more of God's character and grace to others, but we are also called to be receptive to God's wonderful grace, which he is longing to pour out on us; to enjoy his loving kindness and receive his provision. Look out for it today and expect to receive it.

Your companion

66 *Do not let your hearts be troubled.* 99
John 14.1

These words of Jesus imply that we have a choice about whether or not to be troubled by the things that impact on us. After all, it would be very unfair of Jesus to command us to do something that we have no means of achieving.

Anxiety often seems to develop without warning, and certainly without any deliberate choice; something might disturb you and a troubled heart kicks in. How can you change this seemingly natural progression?

The context of this whole section of John's Gospel guides our thinking. The disciples were about to face a troubling time of enormous proportions; everything they believed in was about to be shaken. In preparation for this, Jesus reminded them of the reality of who he was: a reflection of the Father. He went on to reveal that even when he left them, they would have another companion, the Holy Spirit, who is just like him. As they learned to trust their new companion and live in his presence, they discovered they were not alone in the situations facing them, and they could look to the future with a new confidence.

The wonderful assurance that we are all living temples of the Holy Spirit causes this truth to surface once again: whatever you face, you are not alone. In the day ahead, take this truth seriously.

Growing
in faith | 1

Caught in a storm, the disciples feared for their very lives. Jesus calmed the storm, turned to them and asked, "Where is your faith?" There are two ways of interpreting this question, both potentially quite challenging, so we will consider one today and the other tomorrow.

The first interpretation is along the lines of 'how real is your faith in Jesus?' You may profess to believe, attend church regularly, read the Bible, pray and seek to live a life that you feel honours Jesus, but when troubles and anxiety kick in, that is the moment of testing. You might ask why God has allowed something bad to happen, and there can be occasions when this difficult question causes your belief in God himself to waver. At these times, Jesus still asks this same question, "Where is your faith?" Another way of putting it is, "Do you still believe that I am here, and can work something for my glory in this situation?"

All too often it is tempting to feel a failure in the face of troubles. This is simply not true – but perhaps you are being invited to grow in your faith?

Putting your faith in God | 2

"Where is your faith?"

Luke 8.25

This question can be rephrased to mean, 'In what are you putting your faith?' Real hopelessness is when there is nothing or no one in whom you can put your faith. Jesus' constant call is to put your trust in him alone. For example, in terms of health and healing, if you are sick, the call of Jesus is for you to have faith in him. Of course, this does not imply that you should not visit a doctor, but Jesus' call to you is to see the hand of God at work through the medical profession. Far from dishonouring those with medical skills, once their work is viewed as part of God's gift to the world and not just in terms of human standards, they should be held in even greater esteem.

Having faith in God is about coming to him before you seek help from other sources. It might only take a second or two, but in that moment pray along the lines of, 'Through these people and their skills, come to me Lord Jesus.' In this way, whether you are going to the doctor, making an enquiry from an official or facing a tricky situation at work, you will begin to find you are putting your hope in God and not just in other people.

Intimacy with Jesus

Intimacy with Jesus certainly enhances our prayers and provides a real sense of companionship in a world that can sometimes seem hostile – but there is even more. This intimacy is also a means of power to escape the corrupting influence of the world.

One way of thinking of this intimacy is to visualise Jesus as a sealed unit dwelling within you, but the more open, honest and vulnerable you become with him the more his transforming power is able to leak out into you.

It can be easy to think that intimacy with Jesus involves regularly hearing his whispers, but it probably begins with you turning to him frequently, being honest about your feelings and sharing your vulnerabilities. As your intimacy with him increases, so does his intimacy with you and his transforming touch is able to change you.

If a part of intimacy with Jesus involves you being honest and open about yourself to him, what are you going to share with him right now?

Kingdom without end

> *Of the increase of his government and peace there will be no end.*
>
> **Isaiah 9.7**

These wonderful words of hope were spoken by Isaiah as he looked forward to a time in the future when someone new would enter this world, an individual such as the world had never seen before. This was Jesus.

Isaiah's words give us an amazing revelation of the kingdom that Jesus came to bring. Isaiah was stating something far more profound than his belief that there would be no end to Jesus' government. What he actually said was that there will be no end to its increase. In other words, the rule and authority of Jesus increases with every single day.

This is a huge encouragement as we continue to pray for some things on a regular basis while perhaps also fearing that nothing much changes. The truth is that every time you pray for something there is an increase of God's kingdom. You may not see the increase, or it might be of a different nature to that which you were expecting, but this is the truth that Isaiah glimpsed all those centuries ago: there will be no end to the growth of God's reign in your life.

Take heart from this: God's kingdom is increasing through each of your prayers. Recognise that he is at work, and give thanks for his presence in all situations.

> 66*When I called him*
> *he was but one...*99
> **Isaiah 51.2**

It's not because of who we are

These words of God refer to Abraham, and remind us of something very wonderful: Abraham became the father of many nations. In fact, we are told in Genesis 32.12 that his descendants would be as numerous as the grains of sand upon the sea. Yet when God called him it was very different – there was just Abraham. God did not choose him because he had a large family or had proved he was capable of being a good father to many children. When God called him, Abraham was a long way from where God knew he would end up.

The good news is that you, too, may feel as if you are a long way from where God wants you to be, and the distance you need to travel may seem enormous, but that should never cause you to doubt that God has called you. You haven't been called by God because of your achievements, but simply because he loves you. In fact, Paul wrote in Ephesians 1.4 that we were all chosen 'before the foundation of the world', before we were even born and certainly before we achieve anything.

However you feel you are doing, take a moment to reflect on this encouraging truth: it doesn't matter what you think you are achieving, God has put his hand upon you and chosen you, and he knew what he was doing.

God's desire for your life | 1

> 66 *This is how you are to bless the Israelites. Say to them: "The LORD bless you and keep you; the LORD make his face shine upon you and be gracious to you; the LORD turn his face towards you and give you peace."* 99
>
> **Numbers 6.23–26**

Most people who go to church regularly will recognise Numbers 6.24–26, as it is often used as the blessing at the end of services. However, this very familiarity can rob us of the revelation of God's heart enshrined within it. These words, which we will look at over the next few days, are so amazing that it is possible to regard them as wishful thinking, words that we quickly file away in the 'too good to be true' folder.

It is important to note that this first truth, 'The LORD bless you', comes from God himself. The words that follow reflect God's desire and his wish for us; they reveal what God wants to see in our lives.

As with so many promises in the Old Testament, these words were fulfilled by Jesus. Although this blessing was originally given to the Israelites, Jesus is at the heart of it, and all of us who put our faith in him are just as much inheritors of the riches of this blessing as the Israelites. Take a moment to read these verses again slowly. Try to catch the sense that these words are God's words to you and they reveal his heart for you.

There's no exclusion clause | 2

When he gave this blessing to Moses to pass on, God was not fussy about who Moses blessed with it! In fact, he was revealing his heart for all his people.

We can be so quick to assume that God's wonderful promises are for everyone else except us, but this is simply untrue. When God spoke this blessing, he was not thinking of a few particular Israelites, but all of them. He didn't add a clause excluding those who didn't deserve to be blessed; it was for everyone without exception.

It is so easy to think, 'If only God knew what I was really like, surely he wouldn't want such good things for me?' Yet by giving up his life for us Jesus took away everything that could possibly separate us from him. Everything we can think of that might exclude us was taken away because of what Jesus did, so this blessing is for every one of us.

As you read through these words of blessing again, catch the truth that they are for you and you are not excluded. Every time the blessing speaks of, 'the Lord', add the words, 'wants to…' so that it reads: 'The Lord wants to bless you and keep you; the Lord wants to make his face shine upon you and be gracious to you; the Lord wants to turn his face towards you and give you peace.'

God's heart exposed | 3

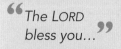

The LORD bless you...

Numbers 6.24

The heart of God is fully revealed here; he wants to bless us. So many people feel God's desire is actually to judge or condemn them. They sense he is indeed with them at every moment, but he is watching them to record every thing they do wrong. Nothing escapes his eye, and they will get away with nothing. This simple statement shatters that picture: God's desire is to bless us, not to record our every failing.

When the Old Testament was translated into Greek, the word used to translate the Hebrew word 'bless' literally means 'to speak well of'. This is the lovely nature of God's desire to bless us. He is not recording our every fault, but speaking well of us.

How do we change our image of God? Take a moment to remind yourself of the truth of the Father's love and that you are his precious child. Ask the Holy Spirit to bring to you a real sense of Jesus with you right now. Whether you feel unworthy before him or not, what do you sense him saying to you?

God watches over me | 4

Once again, we come back to God's heart for us. The word 'keep' contains the sense of guard, preserve or keep watch over. God wants to watch over and preserve what he values, not something he dislikes.

This becomes personal in Isaiah 43.4 when we read that God's people are 'precious and honoured in his sight' and he loves them. This is true for each individual person, not just people in the plural (referring to a whole nation). God included this phrase in his blessing because he wants everyone to know his heart is to keep and preserve each one of his people.

As you spend a few moments sitting before God, take seriously the fact that you are precious to him and say these words slowly to yourself: "I am precious and honoured in his sight and he loves me." Allow that truth to sink in and find the enormity of his heart for you.

Face to face with God | 5

" ...his face... "
Numbers 6.25

There are two references to the face of God in this blessing. A more literal translation of each phrase is:

The Lord, his face to you, shine,
The Lord, his face to you, turn.

In other words, God's blessing to us is in turning his face towards us.

It is interesting to read that Exodus 33.11 speaks of God and Moses speaking 'face to face', but only a little later in verse 20 God says to Moses, "You cannot see my face." This suggests that the phrase 'the face of God' refers to God's actual presence rather than a literal interpretation of it. So when God shines or turns his face to you, things happen.

The presence of God is not a mystical experience that is only experienced by a few people. The gift of the Holy Spirit is the reality of his presence for all of us, and if God is not present, then the Holy Spirit has not been given. It is our belief in the reality of God's presence that is more likely to be lacking.

Worship is a gift to us in such circumstances. We worship an unseen God for his presence among us (which we may not feel), but the more we begin to worship what we do not see and do not feel, the more a different type of awareness comes to us and God's presence becomes a reality. Take a few moments to worship him for his loving presence with you right now.

> **"** *...the LORD make his face shine upon you...* **"**
>
> **Numbers 6.25**

Transforming power | 6

We all enjoy spending time in the presence of God, and when a physical place is deemed to be a place of his presence, people honour that place and flock to it. However, the presence of God is not simply a 'nice' feeling that comes over us at times, or a sensation we seek; it is his transforming power. When God is present, it is with the whole of his heart and all of his power.

In Psalm 80 we read three times, 'make your face shine upon us that we may be saved'. In other words, the expectation is that the presence of God will change things and not just be a comfort in hard times.

When you become aware of the presence of God, whether it simply comes upon you or is something you choose to believe by faith as you worship him, catch the sense that his presence can actually be a transforming presence in your life. With his presence comes his active love and the same heart that caused him to give Jesus so that you might have abundant life.

You may dream of God's transformation in your life, and the good news is that this dream is actually a reality because of his presence within you. Relax in his presence right now and let it bring change to you.

I don't get what I deserve | 7

The grace of God is all about what you do not deserve. Despite anything you have done in your life, and however badly you might see yourself, God is still for you, longing to bless you and shower you with his love. This might be why it is often hard to believe in God's promises. We live in a world where so much of our self-worth is based on questions such as, do I deserve it? Have I worked hard enough? Am I good enough?

What if these were questions God never asked or even thought to ask? This is grace; what God gives is unrelated to what you have done. If you really believe that, what difference does it make to the way you pray?

So what are the questions God asks as he looks at you? They are probably questions more focused on Jesus: did his death release all the blessings, and was his sacrifice enough? The answer is a resounding 'Yes!'

Grace is all about what Jesus has done for you and not what you deserve.

25

Giving joy to God | 8

If the face of God were to be downcast, it would signify his disapproval. Similarly, when the Bible speaks about God's face being turned or lifted to us, it describes his pleasure in us.

Tragically, and all too often, people believe that if they turn to God he will disapprove of them, even though they know he loves sinners and freely welcomes them into his embrace. Sometimes the temptation is to acknowledge that while God may love us we are not too sure if he likes us very much! We are not certain that we match up to his high standards. In the back of our mind lurks an image of a report card saying something like 'could do better'!

If God loved us even before we acknowledged him, how much more is his heart turned to us now that we have accepted his embrace? One of the greatest truths we can learn is that God takes pleasure in us. Any delight we may feel at his presence with us is far outweighed by the joy in his heart when his beloved children turn to him. Take a moment to focus on this reality. Rest in the love that caused Jesus to give himself for you, and find the truth in these words God speaks over you: "In you, I take pleasure."

Our well-being | 9

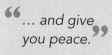

... and give you peace.
Numbers 6.26

Peace can mean different things to different people: a fragile truce, the absence of a storm or a particular feeling. When the Bible speaks of peace, the word 'shalom' carries with it the sense of well-being in every aspect of our lives.

One title that Isaiah gave to Jesus was 'Prince of Peace', and the ministry of Jesus reveals the nature of this peace he came to bring. It is about healing: the healing of our relationship with God, with other people and the healing of our bodies and minds.

When peace is pronounced as a blessing, it is a statement of God's intention and desire for us, that we might receive what Jesus came to bring just as surely as if we were standing before him ourselves.

As you sit quietly for a few moments, let the words of Jesus resonate deep within you: "My peace I leave with you." They are his words to you today.

> *I will never stop doing good to them*
>
> **Jeremiah 32.40**

God never stops doing good

God's wonderful plans for us are that he will never stop doing good to us. However, many of us might be tempted to look back over times in our lives, or possibly things we are going through right now, and come up with plenty of occasions when we have not seen much evidence for this statement. Can God be serious?

It all depends on what is meant by doing good. If it means an expectation that God will do everything we would like him to do, then we might find ourselves disappointed. God doing good to you may involve more than giving you everything you want.

It can be very hard to see the hand of God's blessing in the midst of difficult circumstances, but if you can form a habit of spending time reflecting on the past day and asking yourself where you can see the hand of God at work, you are more likely to be able to see the daily blessings that God pours out on you. What you are likely to discover is that rather than wonder where God was when you really needed him, you will be amazed at the enormity of his activity in your life.

Look back and reflect on the past day. Even if you could not see it at the time, where would you say that you can now see the hand of God at work?

Building faith

> **"**I believe that you are the Christ, the Son of God, who was to come into the world.**"**
>
> **John 11.27**

It is so easy to read the Bible from the perspective of knowing how the story will work out in the end. One way of growing our faith is to see our own lives reflected in the Gospel stories and, knowing what we know about Jesus, trying to respond in the way we feel the people in the Gospel stories should have reacted.

The story of Lazarus is a good example: we know how it ends and are willing Martha and Mary to have faith that Jesus is going to do something wonderful. However, in our own lives we are not necessarily so good at having the faith we want to so easily encourage in others.

Today's Bible passage consists of words spoken by Martha as she made tentative steps towards believing that Jesus was about to do something wonderful. They are words we would all do well to take to heart. As you face situations in which you know you ought to have faith, but don't, try to let her words be your words. Repeat them until you find your faith rising in the truth that Jesus is with you, and his presence can change things: "I believe that you are the Christ, the Son of God, who was to come into the world."

He is mighty to save | 1

The very heart of our hope can be summed up in this beautiful verse: that whatever we are going through, either external difficulties or inward torments, we are not alone. It is also a reminder that the nature of our God, who is with us, is not to sit by casually watching our distress, but to intervene in power and bring change. How can this be more of a reality for us?

One way of seeing the presence of God turned into action is to be more open to the different ways in which his help and salvation might come. The warrior God may well step in and intervene with his mighty sword – or we may be ministered to in a completely different way. The Bible illustrates some of the different ways in which the Lord brings provision. For example, there are several occasions where people are supernaturally fed: in the wilderness, the people of God were fed regularly by manna appearing on the ground; in the Gospels, Jesus fed a large crowd by multiplying food in his hands; and Elijah rested whilst ravens brought him food.

What is your need? It may be helpful to spell it out or, even better, write it down. At the end of the day, or in a week or so, look at what you have written and record on the same page anything that relates to your need being met. In this way, be aware of Jesus, who stands with you and is mighty to save.

I am a delight! | 2

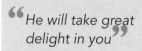

"He will take great delight in you"

Zephaniah 3.17

It is quite easy to see why many people feel that on a good day they might be tolerated by God! There are so many sermons about God's hatred of sin and his wrath upon sinners that it is only natural to assume human beings are not easy to love. Added to that, we are only too aware of our failings so it is easy to catch a sense of his displeasure in us personally.

This view will always prevail if we look at ourselves and our lives first and then go on to build up a picture of God. A far better place to start is by looking at God.

The picture of God presented in the Bible is quite different from the outline above. It speaks of a God who loves us so much he gave Jesus for us; hardly the action of a God who simply tolerates us. Toleration does not lead to sacrificial giving, delight does. When we read that God takes great delight in us, it is his giving of Jesus for us that shows this to be true.

Can you really believe that God delights in you personally? Fixing your eyes on the person of Jesus will reveal this to be true and your desire to encounter him shows your belief in the truth of this.

Take a moment to focus on the Father's pleasure in you, the Father who gave Jesus for you. Then ask the Holy Spirit to bring Jesus to you so you can sit in the company of the one who revealed God's delight to you.

Being truly loved | 3

We often think about love in terms of passion or longing, but to be stilled by love is an extraordinary concept. The sense is that anxiety fades in a loving relationship and a deep peace takes over.

For this to happen, the love relationship must presumably be two-way; to be quietened by love means we need to have a deep knowledge of this love. To *know* we are loved by God is different from being *told* we are loved, and different from *hoping* we are loved. There is a confidence in it.

One way of expressing our confidence in God's love is to worship him, and the more we do this, the more aware of his love we become. In other words, as you begin to worship the Father for his love, you are at the same time acknowledging and thanking him for his love for you. As you step further into this love, your gratitude for it increases, which in turn takes you deeper into it.

Worship God for the depth of his love for you, and find yourself stilled by it.

What makes God rejoice? | 4

"...he will rejoice over you with singing."

Zephaniah 3.17

This verse can help to take our understanding of God's love to a whole new level. It isn't simply a matter of knowing in our minds that we are loved, it is accepting that God rejoices over us with singing! We might rejoice over a sports team that has won a match by singing and chanting, but God's rejoicing over us is not quite the same, since he is not rejoicing because of anything we have done.

Sometimes we see images of wrongly convicted prisoners, or political prisoners, being released to the sound of much joy and rejoicing. There is a real element of truth displayed in this image, as God does indeed rejoice over the freedom Jesus won for us.

However, there is another equally powerful image: of a parent holding a baby and simply rejoicing, even before the child has done anything good, or contributed in some way to the family other than simply being there. This is the rejoicing God has for us. Out of his love he adopted us as his children so that he can pour out even more love upon us. This is his love, and the reason why he rejoices over you with singing.

Recognise this glorious truth – that God sees you as a baby in his arms and rejoices over you.

Am I called?

'Then I heard the voice of the LORD saying, "Whom shall I send? And who will go for us?" And I said, "Here am I. Send me!"'

Isaiah 6.8

What does it mean to have a calling? The idea can summon up dramatic images of God pointing his finger at someone, deliberately and specifically choosing them for a particular purpose.

The call of Isaiah was of a different nature, and is actually far more challenging for us. Isaiah had a vision of God, who simply asked a question, "Whom shall I send?" Isaiah responded by volunteering to be the answer to God's question.

Admittedly, you may not have such a dramatic vision of heaven, but your Bible is full of visions of God enthroned on high. God's throne is not an abstract throne set among the fluffy clouds of heaven; it is set among the reality of human need. Perhaps when some kind of human need grips you that, too, is God saying, "Whom shall I send?"

You obviously cannot do everything, but perhaps you can do something. Take a first step and identify what concerns you. What situation really bothers you? Then consider whether there is anything practical you can do. If there is, think about doing it; if not, take up the cause in prayer.

Catching peace

'While they were still talking about this, Jesus himself stood among them and said to them, "Peace be with you."'

Luke 24.36

There is something wonderful about the fact that when the risen Jesus met his disciples his first words were a desire for them to be at peace. In the light of all that had happened there would have been many things Jesus could have said, but he chose to extend peace to them. These words may have been a common form of greeting, but as we read of the way he dealt with their joy and enthusiasm, it is clear he was delighted to be with them.

What a difference it would make to us if we actually believe that each day when we come to God afresh in prayer the first words Jesus wants to speak to us are, "Peace be with you." You may come to him with anxieties, despair, or maybe a troubled conscience, but before you speak about these things, try to catch his words to you, "Peace be with you." Though he sees exactly what is on your heart, his first desire is that you know his peace.

He is all we want

The Message translation of the Bible translates this verse beautifully: 'Who you are and what you've done are all we'll ever want.'

This sounds wonderful, but is it true? Is it actually true that God is everything you want, or are there one or two other things you would love as well?

When Isaiah wrote these words, he had discovered God was so wonderful that all his other dreams and desires were eclipsed. The question is this, was there something special about Isaiah or could this actually be true for all of us; could God be bigger and better than all your other hopes and dreams? Could he really be so real that he is all you want?

Surely this must be true for us all? Presumably Isaiah was a person with ordinary human dreams and hopes, just like us. What he discovered to be true about God can also become true for us. How do we find it?

So often, when we make a decision that something is true our actual confidence in it follows later and then begins to sink in. Take a few minutes to slowly repeat this phrase to yourself: "All you are and all you have done is all I want." As you say these words, ponder them so they come alive for you, and the reality of God will grow.

Our reputation in heaven

'When Jesus heard this, he was amazed at him, and turning to the crowd following him, he said, "I tell you, I have not found such great faith even in Israel."'

Luke 7.9

Can you imagine spending eternity being known as the person who had the greatest faith? What did this man do to earn such a reputation? The individual in question was a Roman centurion, by all accounts a good man. He was respected by his staff and had a real affection for the nation in which he was stationed.

Yet his goodness is not the reason he is remembered, but rather his faith, which was based not on a startling religious experience but on an unshakeable conviction that Jesus was who he said he was. He reasoned that if this was true, then by the simple application of logic, Jesus would naturally want to help and heal.

You may or may not have had startling religious experiences (you may envy those who do), but in the end what really matters is what you do with the faith you have. Your reputation in heaven does not seem to depend upon what has happened to you in life, but rather on what you have done with it.

Repeat the name 'Jesus' to yourself. He is with you. What difference is this going to make to your day?

> *'... so he was named Jacob.'*
>
> **Genesis 25.26**

Being chosen

The story of Jacob is fascinating. Here was a man chosen and blessed by God to be a central figure in the establishment of God's people, yet all his life he was tricked and cheated and in turn he tricked and cheated others. The footnote in the Bible translates his name as 'he deceives', so he certainly lived up to his name!

He treated his brother with contempt, allowed himself to be swayed by his mother in deceiving his father and always struggled to believe God was with him, so he constantly sought to make blessings become a reality by his own efforts. He really was not the sort of person you would think of as a candidate for blessing and anointing. So why would God use someone like him?

The simple fact is that God chose Jacob regardless of whether or not he would live up to his calling. It was not Jacob's goodness that brought about anything, but the hand of God.

The lesson for us in all of this is that we too are chosen. Ephesians 1.4 speaks of us being chosen before the foundation of the world so, like Jacob, we have not been chosen because of our goodness or saintly behaviour. We are simply chosen by God. What you do with this fact is up to you, but first, rejoice in it. You do not have to battle to get God to choose you, as he has already done that, so relax and see what he can do through you. Bear these words in mind: 'I am chosen.'

Doing good

> " He must turn
> from evil and
> do good "
>
> **1 Peter 3.11**

What are you going to achieve today? It can be a challenging thought that as you live out each day you bring pleasure to God and to others in a very simple way: by doing good.

This command is all about keeping your eyes open for opportunities to perform acts of kindness to others. It may be a small act of kindness for a friend or family member, a comforting word to someone who seems to be stressed or a generous act to a stranger who appears to be in need. It's not just about being nice, but about taking a stand. No matter what may have happened to you in life, no matter how badly people treat you or have treated you in the past, no matter how you may be feeling, Peter points out that God's calling to you is to repay evil with blessing, to do good and act with kindness in all situations.

This is something you can do in any situation in which you find yourself. You can rise above your own feelings and be a blessing to others.

> *...the Holy Spirit descended on him in bodily form like a dove.*
>
> **Luke 3.22**

Living with a dove on your shoulder

Imagine if this were true of us! Just think what it would be like to live with the dove of the Holy Spirit resting on your shoulder. What difference would it make to the way you live? You would probably try harder not to sin and avoid things that the dove would not like.

Communication with this dove would be important, and whether or not he spoke in your mother tongue, you would naturally sense his communication and know whether he was peaceful and at rest, or in a state of agitation and distress. If this dove could speak to you in words, you would probably be extremely eager to hear his voice at every point of the day.

Why not seek to walk through the next 24 hours with an awareness of the dove of the Holy Spirit upon your shoulder? If you are aware of what your actions are doing to him and what he is seeking to communicate to you, your day might well be transformed.

Changing your focus

> *'Alarmed, Jehoshaphat resolved to inquire of the LORD, and he proclaimed a fast for all Judah.'*
>
> **2 Chronicles 20.3**

Jehoshaphat was extremely alarmed when he was told that a vast army was coming against him, but his response was amazing. Rather than make enquiries about the detailed nature of the threat, he turned to God instead.

What we look at becomes magnified in our sight. No doubt if Jehoshaphat had looked more closely at the problem, the details of the attack would have grown even more intimidating; but he made an immediate choice to look to God, and encouraged everyone else to do the same. This resulted in the nature of God being magnified in his sight. In the prayer that follows, he expressed his heartfelt faith when he said, "We do not know what to do, but our eyes are upon you." (2 Chronicles 20.12)

Things happen to us, some dreadfully unfair, but having a problem is not the issue: it's what we do with it that counts. If there is something looming large in your life, turn like Jehoshaphat to God and say, "I do not know what to do, but my eyes are upon you."

'May the Lord direct your hearts into God's love...'

2 Thessalonians 3.5

Walking towards his love

Prayer happens for many different reasons; sometimes out of desperation, often out of habit or duty, and at times out of love. These words, spoken by Paul, point us to another reason why we may be drawn to prayer: by the direction of God himself.

Paul's prayer is that our hearts are directed into God's love. Why would God want us to do this? The fact that God has to direct us suggests we probably would not go there naturally. Our hearts may have a tendency to focus on a sense of God's disapproval or disappointment with us, or an awareness of his demands upon us, when he is actually seeking to lead us elsewhere.

We often use the phrase, 'being open to the Spirit', and this implies a willingness to be open to wherever the Holy Spirit wants to take us. Today's verse reveals that one of the key places the Lord wants to take us is deeper into the Father's love. If we begin to walk down that path, then we can be sure we are co-operating and walking with him. Why not say to God now, 'Lord, lead me into your love for me'?

Discouragement

> *They hired counsellors to work against them and frustrate their plans...*
> **Ezra 4.5**

The background to this verse is that the people had just started to focus on the work of rebuilding the walls of the temple when they met with opposition. It is interesting to note that this opposition did not come in the form of a physical attack, but began in the subtle area of discouragement. The Message Bible speaks of the attempt to 'sap their resolve'. It may have been tough for the workers at the time, but hearing about their difficulty is encouraging for us, because often the battles we have to fight involve standing up to discouragement.

The word 'discouragement' features quite a few times in the Bible, usually in the form of a command about not being discouraged. If this is what we are commanded, then it must be possible for us to obey, and we do not have to listen to the inner voices that are so quick to sap our resolve.

The antidote to discouragement is first and foremost to remember who you are: a temple of the Holy Spirit, in whom he is pleased to dwell, and in whom he takes such great pleasure. Secondly, remember that God is for you (Romans 8.31), so whatever other voices are seeking to discourage you, God is not! He is with you, building you up and offering encouragement.

Take a few moments to dwell on these words: 'God, you are for me.'

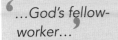

> *...God's fellow-worker...*

1 Thessalonians 3.2

Being God's fellow-worker

Paul uses these words to describe Timothy, but they also describe all of us as we go about our Christian lives.

Your faith is not simply for your own benefit and blessing, it is the good news of God for everyone, and we are all called to work with God in sharing this good news with others. You may feel this is a guilt-inducing challenge, whereas it is actually a wonderful vision of how you can learn to think of yourself.

You have the potential to be a fellow worker with God; the Bible never speaks of different grades of Christian. We all have existing within us the same Holy Spirit who has filled every Christian who has ever lived.

You also have an opportunity. Christians are all filled with the same Holy Spirit, but where they differ is in their personality and the circumstances in which God has placed them. What we all share in common is God's vision of us as his fellow workers.

It is so easy to compare yourself to others. However, God does not do that. He is looking at you – his fellow worker – with pride. What will you do with him today?

The first time – again!

John 7.46

> "No one ever spoke the way this man does," the guards declared.

Interestingly, these words were spoken by the guards who had just been sent to arrest Jesus, but they were so struck by what he said that they came back without doing what they were supposed to do!

How do we react to the words of Jesus? There is a saying that 'familiarity breeds contempt', and while we may not hold Jesus' words in contempt, certainly our familiarity with them can lessen their impact upon us. Similarly, the accounts of the life of Jesus can lose their impact because we know what will happen next.

When you read a Bible passage, try to rediscover a sense of freshness and amazement at Jesus' words by asking yourself, "What would I think if I was reading these words for the first time?" Jesus' words are timeless; it is our reaction to them that can become stale.

Waiting

> *Do not say, "I'll pay you back for this wrong!" Wait for the LORD, and he will deliver you.*
>
> **Proverbs 20.22**

In a way, this verse is all about voices and our choice over which voice to listen to. When something unsettling happens – perhaps someone misjudges us or says something against us – all too often the temptation is for us to lash out. Even if we don't do it verbally, we probably do it inwardly.

This verse from Proverbs assures us that there is another voice, an inner voice, that calls us to restrain ourselves – not simply in refusing to react, but by refocusing our attention on our relationship with God. It is not a call to ignore all manner of things that have come against us, but rather a call to put our trust in the one who will come to our aid.

Unfortunately, the aid or deliverance God brings does not usually smite down our enemies! Rather, it works upon our hearts. More often than not we would rather God vindicated us and in some way punished those who wronged us, but his dream for us is better than that. His dream is that we become like Jesus and reflect him, so that when people look at us they see him.

There will no doubt be times today or in the near future when the temptation is to lash out against someone. Come back to this simple word, 'wait', and let God touch you before you touch others.

We are loved unconditionally

> 66 *As the Father has loved me, so have I loved you.* 99
>
> **John 15.9**

It is easy to gloss over this amazing statement instead of giving it the consideration it deserves. We probably have little trouble believing in the love the Father has for the Son; after all, Jesus revealed a deep bond between them. The Son gave himself totally to reveal the Father's love to us, so it is little wonder the relationship between them is so strong.

However, when it comes to us being loved by Jesus, we probably have to try a little harder to catch it. We can think of some people that Jesus must love – people who have sacrificed everything for him, or given all they have in the service of others – but what about us?

There are no conditions attached to Jesus' statement. He does not say we will enjoy his love if we do certain things, but simply that all of us can enjoy the wonder of the love of God to the extent that he enjoyed it.

It is probably completely beyond us to work out why we are so loved, but we can start to believe it is true. In the quiet now, enjoy this truth and let it change you from within as you focus on these words: 'As the Father loved Jesus, so Jesus loves me.'

Inspired by hope

'We continually remember before our God and Father your work produced by faith, your labour prompted by love, and your endurance inspired by hope in our Lord Jesus Christ.'

1 Thessalonians 1.3

At the beginning of his letter to the Thessalonians, Paul laid out what it was about his friends that really impressed him, and the words he used really do say a lot about them. One of the phrases that stands out is, 'endurance inspired by hope'. Paul seems to be praising the Thessalonians' ability to carry on in the knowledge that their present situation was not all it should have been.

At times we may have a tendency to accept too readily the things that befall us, whereas if we brought hope to these situations we would begin to see them through God's eyes. His joy in creation was looking at it and seeing that 'it was good'. Jesus' mission was that we might 'have life, and have it to the full' (John 10.10). Hope is when we begin to catch this vision for our lives and, holding it in front of us, have the inspiration to endure our present circumstances in the knowledge that there is more.

If you are going through hard times, hold on to this vision that he came to give you abundant life, and allow it to give you hope.

Be ready

'In Damascus there was a disciple named Ananias.'

Acts 9.10

We have no idea what Ananias was planning to do that day, but what he ended up doing was probably beyond his wildest dreams; he went to pray for a man who had been the greatest threat to the church. What's more, this man (Saul) was healed of blindness as Ananias prayed. Not a bad day by anyone's reckoning!

You probably have some sense of what your day holds for you. The challenge we all face is to spend our days with a real awareness of God's presence in our lives, his rule over everything and an openness to his 'nudge', which is his call for us to respond to him. This 'nudge' may not be something big in our opinion, but if God whispers for us to do it, then it is significant in his eyes.

The key to this approach is to be continually open to God. One of the best ways to do this is to develop the practice of speaking the name 'Jesus' whenever you find yourself in 'idle' mode, whether it be walking, driving, waiting or sitting down. His name on your lips becomes a prayer of readiness, turning your attention to him to hear whatever he wants to say to you.

Practise this now by spending time silently speaking Jesus' name, and let it turn your attention to him.

> '...who put their hope in his unfailing love.'

Psalm 147.11

Expect his kindness

The Living Bible translates this verse beautifully, speaking of those 'who expect him to be loving and kind'. It's about us having a wonderful assurance that God's love is constant and personal, not taking it for granted but trusting it will be there for us whenever we need it.

To expect God's kindness and put our hope in his unfailing love is a wonderful way to approach him, either for ourselves or on others' behalf. Sadly, the way we often come to him is with a niggling doubt that he won't hear us, or with a sense that our actions have caused such a gulf between him and us that it is unlikely he will be favourably disposed to us.

To expect his kindness is actually a very bold attitude. It is to take seriously the verse from Lamentations that 'his compassions never fail. They are new every morning' (Lamentations 3.22–23). Whatever the past may have held for you, you can step into this day and the next day expecting his kindness. Whatever you feel you may have done wrong, you need not fear God's bruising hand or punishment but instead the goodness and welcome of the one who longs for you to call him 'Abba, Father.'

Gazing at Jesus | 1

'Let us fix our eyes on Jesus...'

Hebrews 12.2

One of the most exciting invitations in the New Testament is to fix our eyes on Jesus, and we will explore this in more depth over the next few days. The context seems to be that of a race, where the aim is to finish regardless of who gets there first.

The reason you should fix your eyes on Jesus is to set the direction for where you are going. The implication is that you may run towards the wrong thing, or in the wrong direction, if you take your eyes off where you are heading. This is not as obvious as it seems! The Christian faith can quite easily become a different type of race – perhaps a quest for purity or a crusade against injustice. No one is against either of these, but they are not the central core of our faith. At the centre should be Jesus, and if anything else has got in the way of him, or threatens to, then you need to hear again these words from the book of Hebrews, '…fix your eyes on Jesus'.

> '*Let us fix our eyes on Jesus...*'

Hebrews 12.2

Be fixed! | 2

The word 'fix' implies that we must keep looking at Jesus and never take our eyes off him. The trouble is that most of us are not called to a life of prayer 24 hours a day; we have work to do and responsibilities to fulfil. So is this a command we have no hope of ever fulfilling?

The secret is to learn to live in two worlds at once! Coming back to an awareness of the presence of Jesus with you throughout the day is one way of doing this. Begin each morning with some sort of awareness of him, so that each day becomes a fresh revelation of him with you. Then during the day, whenever you remember, try to get used to asking, "Where are you for me now, Jesus?" You may be reminded of what you received from him in prayer that morning, or possibly a completely new sense of his presence.

The aim is to keep drawing your vision back to the central core of your faith – Jesus. He is always there, so find him. He is with you right now, so come back to him and give him your attention.

Pick a verse... | 3

'Let us fix our eyes on Jesus...'

Hebrews 12.2

Another means of keeping your eyes fixed on Jesus is to choose a phrase, a prayer or a Bible verse and focus on it to such an extent that it becomes a part of your life. Many Christians discover the value of doing this, but it may require a little discipline initially. There are a few options: select a verse from your daily Bible reading that particularly strikes you; or simply repeat the name 'Jesus'; or choose a familiar phrase that many traditions within the church find so enriching, such as "Lord Jesus Christ, have mercy on me".

At the start of each day, spend a few minutes allowing this word or phrase to move from your lips into your mind, and then to your heart. Every so often throughout the day consciously call it back to mind, and quite soon you will find it becomes perfectly natural to be aware of it much of the time.

By doing this you will become more conscious of the presence of Jesus with you and your eyes will be drawn back to him.

> *Let us fix our eyes on Jesus...*
>
> **Hebrews 12.2**

Finding Jesus | 4

The people in the New Testament could see and touch Jesus, but since he no longer exists in the physical realm this is a rather strange command from the author of the letter to the Hebrews. However, it's not our physical eyes that are being spoken about here. In Ephesians 1.18, Paul talks about 'the eyes of our heart' being opened; what he speaks about is an awareness beyond physical sight.

As you sit quietly, enjoy thinking about how you are a beloved child of the Father. After a while, ask the Holy Spirit to bring you into the presence of Jesus. You may have a general sense of him being with you, or perhaps a picture in your mind showing something of his presence or even an awareness of his peace with you in your room. This is the opening of your 'spiritual' eyes to his presence.

The Holy Spirit loves to bring us glimpses of the presence of Jesus. We probably couldn't cope with a full revelation of Jesus enthroned at the right hand of God, but we can cope with the sense of him being here with us now. Find him and enjoy being with him.

Friend and Lord | 5

‘Let us fix our eyes on Jesus...’

Hebrews 12.2

The focus of this verse is the person of Jesus; but who is he? It is very easy to build up a selective picture of him. If only one story about Jesus was read, the impression of him would be limited to that one story. Similarly, any subsequent engagement with Jesus in prayer would also be born out of that one particular story of him.

The Jesus we know is glorious; he is present with us now as the closest friend we could find, and yet also enthroned at the right hand of God and surrounded by power and glory. Both of these extremes are combined when we sense his presence with us. All the glory surrounding him on the throne still surrounds him as we sense the gentleness of his presence. When we draw near to him in prayer, all the resources of heaven are as close as he is to us.

To utter the name 'Jesus' is to both summon the gentleness of the one who washed the feet of his friends and also to be summoned to the very throne room of God, where angels cast down their crowns before him.

'Let us fix our eyes
on Jesus, the author
and perfecter of
our faith...'

Hebrews 12.2

Such loving planning | 6

A humbling truth about our faith is that however much you feel you have searched for Jesus, the reality is he has been searching for you so much more. Jesus is the author of your faith: he desired it, dreamt of it and brought it into being. You did not stumble into your beliefs and become a Christian by chance; Jesus planted faith within you. All your life he has been waiting for you to respond to him, and because he is the author of your faith, it must be so precious to him.

You are probably only too aware of your failures and shortcomings, which can make you feel a disappointment to God. At times like this it is so easy to forget the wonder and delight that you bring to Jesus; you are the work of his hands. Of course, you are unfinished and there is still work to do on you, but each day Jesus looks on you with the delight of an artist working on something dear to him.

Our faith is in good hands! | 7

> 'Let us fix our eyes on Jesus, the author and perfecter of our faith...'

Hebrews 12.2

Seeking to live a life worthy of your calling, and yet resting in the presence of Jesus, who is revealed as the perfecter of our faith, might suggest a possible tension.

If you set out to become as holy and prayerful as possible, you will probably fail quite quickly! The intention may be wonderfully noble, but the means to achieving it might be lacking. There is also a danger of becoming quite critical of others who do not seem to share your zeal, even if you are unable to achieve it yourself. However, if Jesus is the perfecter of your faith, he must have a plan or agenda for you, as well as the means for that perfection to grow within you.

The key to this plan is relationship: of you constantly coming back to him and finding the joy of his presence as often as possible. Jesus loves you and stays with you all the time, and the more you fix your eyes on him, the more your faith is made perfect.

Vision

> 'Then the LORD opened the servant's eyes, and he looked and saw the hills full of horses and chariots of fire all round Elisha.'
>
> **2 Kings 6.17**

Elisha's servant had a moment of panic: they were in a fix! He and his master woke up one morning to discover that the town was surrounded by their enemies and, annoyingly for the servant, his master did not seem to be in the least bit worried about the situation. Elisha had an assurance that everything was going to be fine. When the servant persisted in his panic, Elisha prayed for him and things changed. The servant could suddenly see what Elisha had known all along: that as well as being surrounded by the enemy, there were also angelic beings ready to do battle for them.

It is unclear whether Elisha could see these angelic beings or whether he simply knew that God would not desert him, but this passage reassures us that help that we cannot see with our physical eyes is available to us. God has promised his presence with us at all times, and that we have, dwelling within us, his power, which is like the power that raised Jesus from the dead (Romans 8.11). We may not see it, but we are assured it is there.

If we think it would be helpful to see these things, we can: the Bible is our vision, revealing what we cannot see with our physical eyes. Within its pages we gain new confidence in the situations in which we find ourselves. If you are facing something that is causing you confusion or panic, stand back from it for a moment and see it from the perspective of Jesus being with you. Let this attitude impact the way you see your situation now.

If only we knew

> ❛ Jesus answered her, "If you knew the gift of God and who it is that asks you for a drink, you would have asked him and he would have given you living water." ❜
>
> **John 4.10**

If only we knew! This seems to be the sense behind what Jesus said to the woman he met at the well. She would probably have asked for a lot more than physical water if only she knew just who she was speaking to and what he could do for her. This is probably the heart of Jesus for all of us. If only we really knew the nature of the one to whom we pray and what he could give us, it would probably completely change the way we pray.

In one sense, of course, we do know: God is God and nothing is impossible for him. However, the aspect of this truth we so often fail to grasp is just how much God is for us and longing to pour out blessings in abundance upon us. Most of us seem to hold back from believing in the exuberant generosity of God, but the calling from Jesus is clear: put away such things and fix your eyes upon him – if only you knew!

As you come to God today, before you begin to pray for anything specific, remind yourself of just who it is you are praying to and the abundance of life he offers you.

Finding peace

> 'You will keep in perfect peace him whose mind is steadfast, because he trusts in you.'
>
> **Isaiah 26.3**

The English Standard Version of the Bible replaces the phrase 'whose mind is steadfast' with 'whose mind is stayed on you'. The sense is that when we fix our minds on the one whose heart is fixed on us, something of him is able to flow into us. We are told in this verse that by searching for God and fixing our minds on him, we will receive peace, that quality of life desired by almost every person in the world.

Peace is often regarded as what will happen when something else is achieved first, such as when there is no need to worry because there is sufficient money in the bank or when a relationship goes well and becomes a real blessing. So in your search for peace, a good place to start is to bring your concerns to God rather than attempting to meet them without him. He knows your needs and desires and he may or may not want to change them along the way, but the best place to start is to take them to him.

What do you think will help you on the quest to find peace? Come with boldness to God, who loves you and has given everything for you. As you share your thoughts and fix your eyes on God, let something of him touch you and begin to change you.

Graceful conversation

> 'Be wise in the way you act towards outsiders; make the most of every opportunity. Let your conversation be always full of grace, seasoned with salt, so that you may know how to answer everyone.'
>
> **Colossians 4.5–6**

In some situations, you have probably found yourself longing for the right words to say. It might have been as you tried to share your faith or when you wanted to console someone in need.

According to these verses, it is not about opening your mouth and hearing God speak wise words through you, but rather that there is a certain amount of preparation to be done. This involves ensuring that all your conversations sparkle with grace rather than being boastful, arrogant, condemning or judgmental. Then at the moment when wise or compassionate words are needed, your heart will have been prepared with an ease and naturalness, and what is needed will come forth.

Let this practice start right now. Your next conversation does not have to involve sharing your faith in any specific way, but you could make sure that it sparkles with encouragement, interest and grace. It is a choice you can easily make and put into practice, and as you do you might be surprised at what else emerges.

> *" I must preach the good news of the kingdom of God to the other towns also, because that is why I was sent. "*
>
> **Luke 4.43**

Good news

One of the most noticeable points in this statement is the fact that the kingdom of God is good news. So often the message portrayed by the church actually smacks of the opposite and everything comes down to rules.

The reason why the kingdom of God is good news is because it concerns the king, Jesus. Time and again in the Gospels we read of Jesus interacting with people and bringing good news: healing the sick, forgiving the guilty and bringing freedom for the oppressed. It is this same Jesus who is alive today. The issues you are facing are real, but so is Jesus. As he stands with you right now, what would you consider the good news of the kingdom to be? It comes down to this: as you read the Gospels with wonder and delight in what Jesus came to do, what would you like to ask him to do for you?

All too often, we fear he wants us to be miserable, or at least joyful in our miserable circumstances; but what if good news really is good news for you, and he wants to make it a reality in your life? As you stand in the presence of Jesus, who was sent to proclaim good news, what do you want to ask him to do for you?

A very good place to start

There he built an altar to the LORD and called on the name of the LORD.

Genesis 12.8

When you pray, what do you call upon? What is the first thing you summon up and call to mind?

More often than not, it is our mood or our feelings that we focus on, and we let them shape the tone and language of our prayers. They can also have a big influence on the faith behind our prayers, but does this matter? After all, doesn't God hear every prayer and respond with love and compassion no matter how the prayer is phrased?

Interestingly, Jesus did talk about the way we pray and the words we use. He commended persistence and seemed to frown upon babbling! In fact, he gave us what we call the Lord's Prayer as a model for how we should pray to God.

A good starting point in prayer is to call on the name of the Lord, to deliberately turn away from your own feelings and tune in to the reality of the nature of God. You may feel defeated, but God does not. Perhaps you feel discouraged by events, but he isn't. Or it may be that you can't see a way through, but he can.

Before you utter a single word in prayer, put aside your feelings and focus for a while on the wonder of Jesus. Let this perspective shape your prayers that follow.

> *Is any one of you sick? He should call the elders of the church to pray over him and anoint him with oil in the name of the Lord.*
>
> **James 5.14**

Seeking help from others

Most of us probably prefer to struggle along on our own than to ask for prayer. There may be a number of reasons for this: not wanting to bother others with our concerns; a sense that other people are worse off than us; or a decision to hide our weaknesses and needs so as not to appear vulnerable.

The reason doesn't really matter, but James has some clear teaching for us. If we are sick – and he doesn't specify what sort of sickness; it may be physical, emotional, social or spiritual – then we should receive the ministry of others. Part of this is entirely practical; it can be very hard to pray for ourselves when our symptoms are screaming at us. It is also a matter of living in humility and honesty with one another.

Your willingness to receive the ministry of others is what might encourage them to let down their masks and also ask God for help.

God is thinking about me

' *How precious to me are your thoughts, O God!* '

Psalm 139.17

It is not difficult to think of God's thoughts as precious and valuable, but some other translations bring a fascinating insight to this verse. The New Living Translation phrases it, 'How precious are your thoughts about me.' In other words, it is not just the general thoughts of God that are precious, it is also what he is specifically thinking about you.

The very concept of pondering what God thinks about you might be quite alarming! Even if you know he loves you, it can still be unnerving to consider what he might actually be thinking about you. After all, you might not think too highly of yourself, so what must God be thinking? Yet when David had this revelation of God's heart, he recognised that God's thoughts were precious.

A lovely thing that you can do is to stand before Jesus and seek to see yourself through his eyes. It isn't as difficult as you might think! Begin by reminding yourself of some of the great truths: that you were chosen before the foundation of the world, adopted into Father God's precious family and that he willingly gave Jesus to die for you. Now take a moment to stand before Jesus and ask him to show you what he sees when he looks at you. He may speak in the form of a picture, a Bible verse, or even a random thought that seems to drop into your mind.

Find his love for you, and revel in it.

> *Set your minds on things above, not on earthly things.*
> **Colossians 3.2**

Fixing our eyes on things above

Paul's instruction highlights an amazing reality that we too often forget: we are, all of the time, living in the reality of two worlds. There is the world we inhabit and experience through our natural senses, and a spiritual world of which we are equally a part and which is as real as the other world in which we live. However, we touch and experience this spiritual world in a different way, through faith. What does this mean?

Faith can be described in different ways, and one way of viewing it is to choose to believe something you cannot experience with your natural senses. In other words, right now – wherever you are, whatever you are doing and however you are feeling – you are in the presence of God, surrounded by his love and with his attention fixed on you. He's not waiting to see what you will do wrong, but is longing for you to reach out to him and acknowledge his presence.

Simply speaking the name 'Jesus' is enough to proclaim his loving presence with you wherever you are. Where is he for you right now? Set your mind on him and let him invade your world.

Enjoying his promises

> *"What I have said, that will I bring about; what I have planned, that will I do."*
>
> **Isaiah 46.11**

Verses of promise from the Bible can be so comforting but also difficult, especially in hard times when things may seem to be getting worse. During these moments we may be desperate to see the answer to our longings delivered quickly and finally, and yet sometimes it is only by looking back that we can see the hand of God at work.

In the midst of all you are going through now, one thing you can do is hold on to hope – hope to believe there is more for you. Today's verse can help to fan the flame of hope within you, calling you to look again to God's promise of abundant life, which is his plan for you.

God gives his promises to give us hope, so today, as you look ahead to areas of potential struggle and difficulty, fan the fire of hope with these words: 'What he has said he will bring about, what he has planned he will do.'

> *Search me, O God, and know my heart; test me and know my anxious thoughts.*
>
> **Psalm 139.23**

Dealing with anxiety

David shares such lovely revelations about the presence of God in this psalm, and about God's delight in him, and yet at the very end he reveals his vulnerability by admitting to anxious thoughts. Something about this warms us to David, for at times we, too, all struggle with anxious thoughts.

What we do about them is where we might differ from David, who admitted his anxiety to God precisely because he knew the depth of God's love for him. He knew the tenderness with which God cared for him, and in that context he could stand and invite the God he loved to search him and know his anxieties.

David opened up his whole heart to God because he knew that whatever God found would be treated with such love and gentleness. Yet most of us probably don't care to admit our anxieties, even though we may be eaten up with worry.

Standing before Jesus, who perfectly revealed the love and heart of God, may seem brave, but it is also an incredible act of love. Come before him just as you are and say to him something along the lines of, "I stand before you and know that nothing will stop the flow of your love, so here I am with all my anxieties and fears."

We are not in this alone

Temptation can be a very lonely experience. It can often mark the difference between our 'public' face, seen by everyone, and the reality going on inside. We want to keep our temptations private, as we certainly don't want anyone else to know about them, but this struggle can cause us to feel we are the only person with these particular temptations.

> '*For we do not have a high priest who is unable to sympathise with our weaknesses, but we have one who has been tempted in every way, just as we are – yet was without sin.*'
>
> **Hebrews 4.15**

The Bible speaks about the Holy Spirit knowing our every thought (Psalm 139.2). It is this same Spirit who has seen into the mind of every person, and who inspired Paul to write, 'No temptation has seized you except what is common to man' (1 Corinthians 10.13). It is the same Spirit who revealed to the writer of Hebrews that Jesus was tempted in the same ways as us.

The good news in all this is that when you struggle, you are not struggling alone; this is something every person goes through. Surely God will give you the same powers of resistance as Jesus, because if he had 'super powers' to which you have no access, it would be desperately unfair to encourage you to look to him in times of need.

God knows what you are going through and he is longing to help, so be honest with him.

> *...God, who calls you into his kingdom and glory.*
>
> **1 Thessalonians 2.12**

Being led forward

We all live very different lives with our own circumstances and pressures, yet in spite of this we all live with a similar calling upon us. Paul puts it this way in his letter to the Thessalonians: God calls us into his kingdom.

Whatever your situation, there is more that God has for you. You may consider yourself bound by circumstances, but this phrase puts it differently: there is always more of God's kingdom, and you are called to it. Stepping into his kingdom means admitting the situations surrounding you could be different and making a conscious decision to start believing there really is more.

Today, as you face the routine of your daily life or the panic of something that causes you anxiety, spend a few moments putting everything into perspective by repeating these words slowly and with faith: 'God has called me into his kingdom.'

Be salty

> *"You are the salt of the earth."*
>
> **Matthew 5.13**

This is one of the most familiar sayings of Jesus, but what does it really mean and how can it become relevant for us? The Living Bible translates it as this, "You are the world's seasoning, to make it tolerable." The implication is that every one of us can make a difference to those people around us.

So what can you do? What small acts of kindness from you will touch someone's life? What few words can you say to someone in need of encouragement, whether they are serving you in a shop, delivering your mail or sweeping your street? What can you bring to let them know they are recognised for who they are and not just for what they do?

Such acts might cost you nothing more than a few moments of your time, but to those who receive them they can be salt to change them and brighten their day.

Bearing his image

> "Show me a denarius. Whose portrait and inscription are on it?" "Caesar's," they replied. He said to them, "Then give to Caesar what is Caesar's, and to God what is God's."
>
> **Luke 20.24–25**

Jesus faced opposition during his ministry. The context for this verse was when some of his opponents tried to set a trap for him. In a devastating display of wisdom, Jesus dumbfounded his critics, and his words can still say something profound to us today.

Jesus' teaching was based on the belief that if something bears the owner's mark, it belongs to the person whose mark it portrays. It should not be stolen or defaced because it belongs to someone else.

We all bear the mark of God: we are created in his image and we bear his name. We do not belong to ourselves, we belong to him. The wonderful thing about this is that we have a worth that has been set by him and not by us.

You may see yourself as small in comparison to others, but God has set a value on you which you have no right to challenge or deface; he values you so much that in his eyes you were worth the death of Jesus. Hold in your mind the image of Christ on the cross – in God's opinion, you were worth this.

The beginning of prayer

'But I, by your great mercy, will come into your house'

Psalm 5.7

Two great truths are high-lighted in this phrase. The first is that prayer is not simply about a muttering of words or a silent longing going through our minds. It begins (or at least it can do) with the attitude that we are stepping into his presence. This is true whether we do anything about it or not, but how wonderful to actually take the time to make it a reality for us.

The second truth is that we can come into the presence of God through grace, which has already been poured out. In other words, we can trust that as we turn to God in prayer it is his delight and pleasure that we are in that place because he has opened every door for this to happen. So before you utter a single word in prayer, pause to remember where you are – you are in the very presence of God – and why you are there – because he has gone before you and opened the door.

Now you can begin to pray with confidence!

> " *...for the LORD searches every heart and understands every motive behind the thoughts.* "
>
> **1 Chronicles 28.9**

He sees your heart

A sudden surge of panic may arise after reading these words! It's not always a good thing that God knows absolutely everything!

We often feel we ought to strive to be perfect, as well as highly successful in our lives and in everything we do for the Lord. However, the reality can be quite different, with our prayer times feeling as if we are talking to a brick wall and our attempts at evangelism leaving us wondering why we bother. It can be very easy to feel a bit of a failure.

At times like these, this verse can be such an encouragement because it explains that God looks at the heart behind our actions, not simply at the results. If you pray for something because you long to see God bringing about transformation, he knows about it. When you speak about Jesus, often in ways outside your comfort zone, he also sees this. At times when you long to pray but find it so hard, he is well aware of the desire of your heart.

We are so quick to convince ourselves that God is against us, when the truth is he loves us and appreciates every faltering attempt to bring his glory to this world.

'Lord, you know my heart.'

Jesus in the pain

This is a strange verse if you stop to think about it. Lazarus, a good friend of Jesus, had indeed died, so no wonder Jesus and others felt grief and pain, but we have already been told earlier in the story that Jesus knew what he was going to do. He was about to reveal the glory of God by calling Lazarus from the grave. So, knowing this, rather than weeping surely a more fitting reaction from Jesus would have been joy and worship in the power of God that was about to be demonstrated?

However, Jesus' tears show us something extraordinary about him: they reveal his ability to fully enter into the reality of the situation despite what he planned to do to transform it. Even though he was about to perform an astonishing and transforming miracle, he could still feel the pain of the situation.

As you think about yourself and what you might be going through, know that Jesus cares about it and is fully able to enter into the pain of your feelings. He may be about to do something wonderful and he may be asking you to exercise trust, but he never ceases to see and care about your pain.

14 JUNE

> *But one thing I do: Forgetting what is behind and straining towards what is ahead, I press on...*
>
> **Philippians 3.13**

Don't go there!

How can we forget what is behind us? Sometimes the things from our past are so huge and the memories so powerful that it seems ridiculous to be encouraged to forget them. Chance would be a fine thing!

Paul's word, which is translated in our Bibles as 'forget', has another suggested meaning, that of neglect. In other words, our attitude towards the past should simply be to not go there; don't revisit and dwell on any pain. This advice to forget what might seem unforgettable might sound impossible, but it does begin to be a possibility when taken together with the second part of Paul's advice: to 'strain towards what is ahead'. In the next verse, Paul goes on to explain that our vision should be on the truth, that we belong to a different world.

Jesus is here with you now, so try to find his presence. If you are aware of what you have done in the past, or what the past has done to you, take a few minutes to quietly speak Jesus' name, because in doing this you are speaking to him in the present. You don't even have to say anything specific, just let his name become part of your breathing. As you speak to him you are connecting with him, and your vision will begin to be turned from your past to the future.

The right attitude

Then Jesus said, "Did I not tell you that if you believed, you would see the glory of God?"

John 11.40

Some people can live through, what might seem to us, a fairly normal, routine day and yet see the majesty of God in almost every situation. Others can stare wonders in the face and be totally unmoved. Attitude is what makes the difference. Is your attitude open to the wonders of God, or is it more of an assumption that nothing particularly special will happen today?

Some traditions of the Christian church encourage the practice of constant prayer. The basic idea is that a phrase such as, 'Lord Jesus Christ, have mercy on me, a sinner' (or a version of this) is repeated prayerfully until it becomes part of your breathing pattern. This probably doesn't happen immediately, but with perseverance it is amazing how quickly you can find these words popping into your mind throughout the day, which greatly increases your consciousness of Jesus.

Along with this growing awareness of Jesus comes an increased perception of his activity in your life, which results in your vision of God's glory growing as well. As you breathe in whisper, "Lord Jesus Christ," and as you exhale say, "Have mercy on me."

The fruit of the Spirit | 1

Belief in God is not extraordinary: many people claim belief in some sort of higher being. However, belief becomes more personal when the nature of this higher being is considered. In other words, what is God like?

Over the next ten days we are going to look at the nature of God from what might seem a surprising passage: the verses in Galatians where Paul describes the fruits of the Spirit. These fruits are more commonly thought of as characteristics of what Christians should be like; a description of what the Spirit produces within us. This list of characteristics, however, is more than this. It is also a description of the Spirit himself.

Any fruit must bear a resemblance to the tree from which it comes; an apple tree cannot produce bananas! So in looking at the fruits produced by the Spirit, they must by their very nature be saying something about the nature of the Holy Spirit himself. As we look at the fruits in this light, we discover something beautiful about the nature of the Spirit of God. Rather than being someone who is out to condemn and convict, he is a person of joy and peace living within us.

God's Spirit of joy and peace is with you now; welcome him and begin to relax in his presence.

The love of the Spirit | 2

'But the fruit of the Spirit is love'

Galatians 5.22

The love of the Holy Spirit isn't something we usually think about. We talk of the Father's love and the love of Jesus, but not really the love of the Holy Spirit. However, if love is something the Holy Spirit produces within us, it must also be a natural part of his being.

It is an amazing thought that the Holy Spirit loves us. He was not sent kicking, screaming and full of resentment to live within us, nor does he spend the entire day shaking his head in despair at his misfortune at having to spend years in our company! The Spirit loves us and it is his pleasure to dwell within us. He is thrilled when we turn to the Father's love for us, joyful when we look to all Jesus did on the cross and delighted when we admit our need of him and call on him.

Take a moment to acknowledge the wonder of the love of God that dwells in you right now. His primary role is not of one who convicts but rather the one who loves.

But the fruit of the Spirit is...joy

Galatians 5.22

The joy of the Spirit | 3

We have more than a happy glow when the presence of the joyful Spirit is within us. Nehemiah 8.10 tells us that 'the joy of the LORD is your strength'. We can experience this joy, which is such an integral part of the Spirit's character, precisely because he lives within us.

Presumably the joy which the Spirit bears stems from his intimate relationship with the Father and Jesus. This relationship has given him an understanding of how the Father's presence permeates everything because he is the Lord of all creation, and also the far reaching effects of Jesus' cross and resurrection in every part of our lives. He can see everything.

The presence of the Holy Spirit within us is our ultimate cause for hope, because he knows that everything will be fine in the end. He brings the love of the Father and the work of Jesus to us, and his joy comes from knowing the wonder of God far more than we ever could. This is why his joy is our strength.

Seek to catch something of the Holy Spirit's joy over you now, as he sees far more of God's activity in your life than you ever could.

The peace of the Spirit | 4

'But the fruit of the Spirit is...peace'

Galatians 5.22

It's a wonderful thought that the Spirit who produces peace must himself be at peace within us. If we are honest, our tendency may be to think of the Spirit as one who is constantly chivvying and anxiously reminding us of all we need to know, wondering if we will ever learn or improve beyond where we are.

However, the Spirit is peace and because of this the more you can tune into him, the more his peace is able to flow through every part of you. A good way of doing this is to choose to believe he is at peace within you. Conversely, if you choose not to believe this, you will find yourself fighting him and his nature.

God loves you and delights in you; out of his love he has sent his Spirit to dwell in you and to bring you every good thing he has for you. When we believe the Spirit is on the look-out to condemn us, we must grieve him terribly. He is actually longing for us to catch the fact that he is perfectly at peace with us.

As you say these words, say them in time with your breathing: "The Spirit of God is peace within me."

The patience of the Spirit | 5

What a relief to know the Spirit within us is patient! Impatience and desperation are terms we might be tempted to think of as his feelings towards us. His patience stems from the fact that he loves us and because he has the joy of seeing at first-hand the wonders of God.

His patience probably also stems from the fact that you are not the only human being he has ever dwelt in, and he has seen everything before. He has accompanied people like you through situations just like those you face. What may be a new experience and constitute a crisis for you is not utterly bewildering for him. He has literally seen it all before.

Another reason for the Holy Spirit's patience is because he is totally at peace with who you are and doesn't wish that you were someone else; he is committed to letting you grow and develop into the unique person you are. He is patient, and for him you are worth the wait.

Hold on to this reassuring truth that the Holy Spirit doesn't want you to be just like someone else, but is longing for you to become more like the unique person God created you to be.

The kindness of the Spirit | 6

'But the fruit of the Spirit is…kindness'
Galatians 5.22

Kindness is a beautiful word. We are used to thinking about the love of God, but the word 'kindness' adds something extra to the list of God's attributes. At the heart of it is a sense of goodness, mildness and pleasantness, which reassures us that we want to be with the Spirit and not flee from him.

Sometimes you may wonder whether you would be desperately uncomfortable in God's presence because he is so holy, but a story in Luke 7 reveals his holiness is not like this. It is the account of the woman who wet his feet with her tears and dried them with her hair. We are told that she was indeed a 'sinful' woman, but this didn't make Jesus unapproachable for her; she clearly felt able to approach him in a close and intimate way.

So it is with the Spirit who lives within us. If he produces kindness within us, then he is kind in himself; he is approachable and caring, not fierce and condemning. The Spirit who dwells within you is happy to be there, despite how you view yourself, and he longs for you to respond to his kindness and not fear his disapproval.

> *But the fruit of the Spirit is...goodness*
>
> **Galatians 5.22**

The Spirit within us is good | 7

'Good' is a very over-used word that is applied in a variety of ways, but it is an excellent description of the Spirit who dwells within us. The Holy Spirit is in every way good to us: he thinks good of us, wants good things for us and longs for us to relax in the knowledge of his goodness. We are probably more used to thinking of the Holy Spirit as a disciplinarian who wants to bring us to heel so that we walk the straight and narrow path. Indeed, God is constantly seeking to teach us to keep to his ways, but not with a whip.

The goodness of the Spirit makes such a difference to us when we perceive we have failed in something. A disciplining Spirit would berate us for our failure and tell us we will never succeed at anything. However, the good Spirit loves our efforts, and rejoices when we turn back to him so he can pick us up when we stumble and guide us back to the path.

If you are able to trust in the goodness of the Holy Spirit within you, it will make all the difference as you seek to walk the life he offers. Perhaps what it says most of all is that he is on your side, caring and looking out for you in ways you can't even imagine, and longing to bring more blessing and love to you.

The faithful Spirit | 8

'But the fruit of the Spirit is . . . faithfulness'

Galatians 5.22

The quality of faithfulness carries with it a sense of reliability; it speaks of constancy and consistency in spite of the circumstances. In order to develop faithfulness in others, the Holy Spirit must be faithful himself in spite of whatever else is going on – namely, us! – around him.

We may not be faithful or consistent in the outworking of our faith, but the Holy Spirit is faithful within us, always present, loving and tender despite what we may perceive as our many failings and ways we feel we let God down. The faithfulness of the Spirit is his commitment to our transformation, which he must so desperately long for, but for which he is willing to wait and tenderly bring about at the right time.

When we trust in the faithfulness of God and his Spirit within us, repentance becomes something we can do with boldness and confidence. He will not leave us or clobber us, but waits with love for us to turn to him and find the peace he is longing to give us.

> *But the fruit of the Spirit is... gentleness...*

Galatians 5.23

The gentleness of God | 9

The gentleness of the Spirit, which is also a part of his nature, speaks of the wonder of his approachability.

If you had a deep, dark secret that you had to share, it is likely you would choose someone who exuded gentleness. Gentleness is a quality that makes it possible to share deep things, to draw alongside someone in what might be an uncomfortable time, and to be certain that whatever is said will be spoken with tenderness and a deep love.

Such is the nature of the Holy Spirit within you, and such is the nature of God from whom the Spirit proceeds. Your belief in the gentleness of God can be measured by your willingness to be utterly honest with him about the deep things in your life.

Let the truth of this fill your mind for a few moments as you sit in his presence. Dare to trust his gentleness as you begin to share some things with him that perhaps you have been unwilling to do before.

The choices
God makes | 10

'*But the fruit of the Spirit is . . . self-control.*'

Galatians 5.23

The self-control of the Holy Spirit may initially conjure up an image of a puritanical figure denying himself – and presumably us – any pleasure, but when that self-control is explored, something beautiful begins to emerge.

Self-control is all about making choices to act and behave in a certain way, and behind these choices is a conviction, a real heartfelt desire, to act in a certain way.

All the things we have been considering over the past days in connection with the fruits of the Spirit are the choices that make up part of the Holy Spirit's self-control. He continually chooses to be loving, joyful, peaceful, patient, kind, good, faithful and gentle. He makes a deliberate choice to be like this in spite of anything we may do to tempt him to act differently: however we are, he chooses love; whatever we bring to him, he chooses gentleness; however much we wander away, he chooses faithfulness.

Part of the nature of our faith is to trust in his choices towards us. This doesn't mean we can take his love for granted (we still respond with wonder and gratitude) but we come to him, trusting and relying on his choices. Our response to his presence within us is based on our knowledge of them.

Take a few moments to respond to the nature of God which is revealed by the Holy Spirit. The best way of doing this is to begin to believe it, and to approach God with the same longing that he has for you.

Our attentive God

> *Now my eyes will be open and my ears attentive to the prayers offered in this place.*
>
> **2 Chronicles 7.15**

The context of this verse is that Solomon had just dedicated his newly built temple to God and that very night God delivered his view and vision of it, including his intention to be attentive to the prayers offered there.

When Paul spoke about the nature of Christians, he spoke about us being 'temples of the Holy Spirit'. Since he was well versed in the Old Testament, Paul would not have used the phrase lightly, but would have had a real awareness of the significance of the Old Testament temple as a place to which God was drawn and attentive.

We are his temples now, and God is attentive to the prayers offered within us. He hears everything we say, and knows the dreams and suffering behind these words. So often we think our prayers are not 'getting through', being ignored, or even that God, for some perverse reason, is doing the exact opposite of what we pray.

Let the truth of this verse sink in and know that out of his amazing love for you, God is attentive to your prayers; he listens and hears everything.

"God, your eyes are open to me, and your ears attentive to my prayers."

Keep focused on this

'Each one should test his own actions. Then he can take pride in himself, without comparing himself to somebody else'

Galatians 6.4

Comparing yourself to others is such a harmful activity; it is one of the quickest ways of negating the wonderful things God is doing in your life. To be fair, we can get quite a bit of help with this habit. Many times throughout our lives we have probably been compared to others, and may well have not come off that well.

Each of us as individuals bears the presence of God. He has chosen to put his Holy Spirit within every one of us. It is an act of disrespect and ingratitude to God to disregard this or to let the comments of others rob that uniqueness from us.

As you take a moment to sit before him and remind yourself of his presence within you, focus on the truth of these words, 'I bear your name, O LORD God Almighty' (Jeremiah 15.16). This begins in the singular and means not just other people, but you as well. Despite all that might have been said about you and all you think about yourself, you really do bear that unique touch of his presence upon your life.

No one can ever take this truth away from you, but you can take your eyes off it.

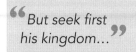

> *"But seek first his kingdom..."*
>
> **Matthew 6.33**

First things first

There are countless times when we simply do not know what to do. You have probably been talking to someone or listening to their story when it has struck you that you simply do not know what to say to them.

This simple, well-known phrase sets out God's agenda – seek first his kingdom – and it should, as it says, be the first thing we do in any situation. What God wants for every one of us, in all circumstances, is to actively seek his rule over the events before us.

Put like that it sounds deeply challenging, and it probably conjures up all sorts of images of you being asked to do things beyond your natural inclinations and abilities. But is it that frightening? Seeking God's kingdom is really a matter of silently praying in as many situations as possible: 'Jesus, how can I bring something of you into this situation?' His answer will probably come as a random thought that goes through your mind, and the thought may be as simple as saying a kind word, offering some encouragement or saying a prayer for a person. Ask the question, let Jesus speak to you, and through all of us the kingdom of God will grow.

God sees things differently

'Great is our LORD and mighty in power; his understanding has no limit.'

Psalm 147.5

This verse might seem like an obvious statement, but the implications of it are enormous for us, especially the phrase, 'his understanding has no limit'. It is precisely our limited understanding that causes us so many problems when it comes to trusting God, because we have no idea how he will work. This lack of vision about what God can do causes our trust to dwindle.

However, the fact that his understanding has no limit means that there is nothing about your situation of which he is unaware, nothing about any contributing factors that he is unable to see and also that there is no limit to his vision of what could happen. Unless you understand this, trusting him is always going to be difficult. It is natural to put your trust in what seems real, and if the possibility of what God can do is not real, how then can you trust in what seems unreal or unreasonable?

If you are facing a difficult situation at this time, honesty is entirely appropriate – as long as you are honest about the unlimited nature of God's vision for your life as well. Let these words go through your mind for a few minutes as you contemplate your immediate situation, and let them enlarge your vision of what he could do: 'You see this situation in a different way than I do.'

Waiting for the touch of God

> *Ten days later the word of the LORD came to Jeremiah.*
>
> **Jeremiah 42.7**

In this particular story, Jerusalem had been captured and most of the people exiled, leaving only a few folk behind. These people came to Jeremiah and asked him to seek the Lord on their behalf about what they were meant to do next. Presumably they sensed Jeremiah was a man of God with a reputation for hearing the voice of God in a much clearer way than they could. Jeremiah agreed to ask the Lord for them, but interestingly the word of God only came to him after ten days.

We live in an age where we expect everything to happen immediately, including answers to our prayers, and if they are not answered quickly then we assume God has forgotten or is not interested. Yet even Jeremiah, as close and intimate with God as he was, waited ten days for God to speak to him.

If you are in a period of waiting for God to speak or act and nothing seems to be happening, then be encouraged and do not assume God is either silent or disinterested. This can be particularly tempting in the area of healing, as each day that healing does not happen the assumption is that it is less likely to occur in the future. This is not true; God has simply not spoken or acted yet, or he may be doing something in another area of your life first. It certainly need not imply you are at fault in any way.

The Father's work

> 'Jesus said to them, "My Father is always at his work…"'
>
> **John 5.17**

God, our loving father, is always at his work of loving, saving and caring. What's more, nothing you do or don't do will alter this fact one jot. Whether you have been active or inactive in your Christian life or faithful or unfaithful in your prayers, he is still at work.

Although we should be committed to our times of prayer, it is possible to get caught up in carrying other people and persisting in prayer for things we do not yet see and then begin to feel that a positive outcome depends on us and our prayers. This, in turn, can cause feelings of guilt when we forget or are too busy to pray, or simply get overwhelmed by it all.

For this reason, we need to come back to the wonder of the presence of God on a regular basis, sitting in his presence and being reminded that the activity is his and all the glory belongs to him.

Take a moment to relax from all your praying and rejoice in the Father's love for you; let the Holy Spirit reveal the nearness of Jesus to you – and enjoy his presence.

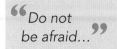

> **"** *Do not be afraid...* **"**
>
> **Deuteronomy 3.2**

It's all a matter of vision

In the first three verses of this chapter, Moses is recounting the story of the encounter between the Israelites and King Og. It began with Og assembling his whole army and marching out to meet the Israelites. Imagine the terror of standing to watch an army advance in front of you, intent on your destruction!

However, God told Moses something which had a transforming effect upon the situation: he had already handed the whole of Og's army over to Moses. With this in mind, the Israelites attacked the army of Og and won a resounding victory.

This victory all started with vision. The Israelites changed from seeing the situation through a vision of fear to seeing it through God's vision.

You may not have to face armies today, but as you look forward to what lies ahead in your life, what are the things that stir up fear or anxiety within you? As you ponder them, ask the Holy Spirit to give you his vision for those moments; what will he be doing and what is he seeking to give you?

As you walk into those moments with his vision, as opposed to yours, everything can change.

Getting our needs met

> *I pray that out of his glorious riches he may strengthen you with power through his Spirit in your inner being, so that Christ may dwell in your hearts through faith.*
>
> **Ephesians 3.16-17**

The concept of Christ dwelling in our hearts is probably something we take quite lightly, thinking of it as a lovely description of his presence with us. It is this – and more. When Christ dwells in us, so does everything that is a part of him: peace, power, love, strength, endurance, grace, oneness with the Father and so on.

We all have needs, and we can spend a considerable amount of time being only too aware of them. Problems can arise when we begin to look for answers to them in inappropriate ways. However, our perspective changes when we begin to see that we already have the answer to our needs in the person of Jesus, who dwells in us.

If you are aware of a genuine need right now, don't try to deny it. Instead take a moment to lift your eyes from your need and, in whatever way you can, find the presence of Jesus with you. Fix your eyes on him and let his presence be a reality for you. What does Jesus have that you need right now? If he has it and he is in you, you have whatever you need within you, so begin to give thanks for it.

Act or react

"*Surely God is my salvation*"

Isaiah 12.2

Perhaps one of the most common mistakes we make as Christians is that we tend to react rather than act. Something either major or quite trivial may happen and rather than approach it in a manner consistent with our faith, our tendency is to react to it with inappropriate emotions, often without much faith and usually with regret!

It would be wonderful if we used these words from Isaiah as a filter for our thoughts and emotions, that whatever happens to us or around us, we can say, "God is my salvation." He is our help, our way out of trouble, and his strength will give us what we need.

It is true that to pray everywhere all the time means that we have to pray somewhere some of the time. The same is true of the Bible verses we want to be familiar to us in times of need; we have to store them up.

Take these words, "God is my salvation", and sit quietly repeating them over and over to yourself. As you do this, let the hours ahead of you come under the truth of them. Then come back to them again throughout the day.

Rejoicing in his love

' For the LORD takes delight in his people.... Let the saints rejoice in this honour...'

Psalm 149.4–5

Things in which we take pleasure or delight bring us joy, and simply looking at them and touching them brings pleasure to us. The psalmist speaks of God viewing his people in the same way: looking at us brings pleasure to God and being in our company brings him delight.

This is so far removed from what we often suspect God thinks of us. Many people think they disgust God, that he is angry with them or simply tolerates them, so it is hard to grasp this revelation that he delights in us. In fact, the reason it has been revealed to us is probably because we would be unlikely to catch it ourselves.

Most of the time we do very little with this truth, probably because we cannot believe it! The psalm encourages us to rejoice, exult and become jubilant. So why not pause for a moment to let this truth sink in: God delights in you, he actually takes pleasure in you. Then in whatever way is natural to you, rejoice in it, take it seriously and express to him how this makes you feel.

Christ over all

> *And he is the head of the body, the church; he is the beginning and the firstborn from among the dead, so that in everything he might have the supremacy.*
>
> **Colossians 1.18**

If you were to take these words seriously, your response could certainly not be, "So what?" Jesus oversees everything you do; he has gone before you into every dark place and has experienced first-hand the wonder of God's transforming power. In every situation, he is Lord.

Whatever the next 24 hours hold for you, the prospects have got to improve if all the above is true because Jesus is there. He who has supremacy over everything will be in each situation that you face. If you can lift your eyes to see things through this perspective, then your day should begin to look a little different.

Perhaps the key is your awareness of it. Take five minutes now to slowly and thoughtfully say the name 'Jesus'. If you follow this practice for a few days, the effect will be that your mind returns to his name increasingly throughout the course of each day, and with an awareness of his name comes the reality of all that he is for you in whatever you do.

Encouragement

> *Let us not give up meeting together ...let us encourage one another*
>
> **Hebrews 10.25**

The writer of Hebrews has been encouraging his readers to come to God, who has done so much for them. In this verse he reminds us that our faith is not a solitary matter. Instead it is something we share with others, and each one of us has our own part to play in relation to the body of Christ. One of these is encouragement.

You will probably come across other people today and have a chance to speak to them, whether they are known to you or strangers. Most people need encouragement, and they thrive on it. This is not just saying something nice for the sake of it, but it involves asking yourself what you can genuinely say to affirm them in something they do. If someone is important to you, tell them why; if they are always there for you, tell them how much it means to you.

Finally, learn to receive the encouragement of others for yourself. It can be all too easy to dismiss it and pretend it's not needed. Instead, treat it as a gift and don't throw it away.

> *...Jesus Christ, who is the faithful witness*
>
> **Revelation 1.5**

What is God like? | 1

Some incredible statements about Jesus feature in this verse and the next, and we will be looking carefully at them over the next few days. This first statement begins by describing Jesus as 'the faithful witness'.

The full and perfect revelation of the nature of God can be seen in Jesus. Many people don't have a problem believing in God, but aren't sure what he is really like. This verse reveals that according to the Bible, Jesus reveals God perfectly.

Every story about Jesus – the work that flowed from his hands and each time he spoke – reveals something about God. Indeed, a wonderful exercise is to take any story from the Gospels and ask yourself what Jesus is showing you about God.

It is interesting that Jesus is described not just as a witness, but a faithful witness. In other words, he chose to reveal God. Presumably he could have been an unreliable witness if he had wished, but such was his knowledge of the wonder of God that he deliberately chose to perfectly and faithfully reveal him, because there could be no better way for us to see and understand what God is really like.

Why not turn to a story about Jesus in the Bible and give some thought to what Jesus is choosing to reveal to you today about God.

Jesus is alive | 2

'...Jesus Christ, who is...the firstborn from the dead'

Revelation 1.5

The resurrection of Jesus is an incredible event that affects us profoundly, and this phrase tells us why. Jesus is described as the firstborn from the dead – it is us who come after. In other words, because Jesus was raised from the dead there is a promise that we will share in that resurrection. We are sharing in it already.

We can rejoice with genuine hearts that we need not fear death; Jesus has been raised from the dead and has gone ahead to prepare a place for us. Death is not the end for us, for beyond it lies a life with Jesus.

However, our faith is not simply about comfort when we die; the resurrection of Jesus also has a profound effect upon us in this life. In the letter to the Hebrews, Jesus is said to have 'the power of an indestructible life' (Hebrews 7.16). In other words, we share in his resurrection by having access to the one who cannot be contained by death.

When you pray, the one who is there for you is the one who has conquered death itself and even a grave could not restrict him.

Jesus is king | 3

> ❛ ...Jesus Christ, who is ... the ruler of the kings of the earth. ❜

Revelation 1.5

To some extent, we are all at the mercy of other people. Sometimes you may feel this more keenly, particularly if you feel subject to discrimination, prejudice, ignorance or misunderstanding, and it can feel as if you have nowhere to turn.

To say all you have to do is pray can sound like a bit of a cliché, because you may have turned your heart to prayer many times. However, there is something you can do before you pray: begin to dwell on the person of Jesus enthroned on high. It is always good to be aware of the reality of Jesus understanding and caring for you right now, but it is also good to gaze upon the truth that Jesus is also enthroned on high. He reigns above every other power, and everything is beneath his feet. This is the Jesus who is with you in your troubles, the one who has the power to sustain you and lift you up.

Before you pray, take a few moments to fix your eyes upon Jesus on the throne, and see your lives and troubles from his perspective.

What is God's love like? | 4

Our focus over the past few days has been some glorious aspects of Jesus: Jesus, the perfect revelation of God; Jesus risen from the dead; and Jesus, ruler over all things. Some of these images are easy to hold in our mind, often thanks to paintings and works of art that reveal different aspects of Jesus. However, the description of Jesus we come across today is beyond depiction: the fact that he loves us.

What is love? Perhaps one of the most powerful descriptions contained in the Bible is Paul's writing in 1 Corinthians 13. These words can be so challenging as we face up to how far we fall short of them. However, another way of reading this passage is to see in the words a description of God's standard of love – a love that must be a description of himself.

Spend a moment reading 1 Corinthians 13.4–7. Take each phrase and word slowly and thoughtfully, not analysing whether or not you match up to the words, but rather seeking to catch the nature and truth of what it means for God to love you in this way.

> *...Jesus Christ...has freed us from our sins by his blood*
>
> **Revelation 1.5**

Freedom | 5

What do you understand by the word 'forgiveness'? More often than not, we think of in terms of Jesus taking the punishment for what we have done wrong. However, this phrase takes forgiveness a step further: it speaks about it in terms of freedom. Freedom is more than being released from God's punishment for our sins, it also implies freedom from the pull of sin upon us.

Our problem is that we don't always feel as if the pull of sin has been eradicated from our lives, but feelings can be deceptive. We believe feelings reveal to us what is true, and of course sometimes they do. However, sometimes what they reflect is the nature of temptation. You may feel a desire to do something, but that does not mean you have to do it.

This phrase from Revelation reminds us of the fact that when Jesus died the price of our individual sins was forgiven. Something more profound also took place: our sinful nature died with him. You may still be tempted to do wrong, but you do not have to follow your feelings. You have been set free. Take a minute to let the truth of this sink in: 'I am free!'

You matter to God | 6

'...Jesus Christ...
has made us to
be a kingdom...'
Revelation 1.6

We are a kingdom. We have Jesus as our king and we are the ones for whom Jesus is pleased to be king. Jesus has made all of us to be a kingdom – not just the strong, mighty warriors for the Lord who blaze a trail for Jesus wherever they go, but also those of us who are struggling to know whether God could ever love us.

Sometimes a sense of our own unworthiness consumes us to the extent that we are robbed of any sense of our value to God, and God is robbed of the joy of knowing we take as much pleasure in him as he does in us.

Jesus has made us to be a kingdom, but he is not sitting in heaven regretting his mistake! He is pleased with his choice so we can hold our heads up high, knowing we are loved and chosen and we belong to him.

Take a moment now to ponder this wonderful truth that you are his and he takes pleasure in you. You matter to him and he wants you to grasp this and open yourself up to the sense of his pleasure in you.

> '...Jesus Christ...
> has made us to be...
> priests to serve his
> God and Father.'

Revelation 1.6

Bringing pleasure to God | 7

Jesus making you a 'priest' might seem quite an odd concept. Actually, it is a word that speaks of the high calling you have and the regard Jesus has for you.

Throughout the Old Testament, the main function of a priest was to bring pleasure to God by ensuring the correct sacrifices were offered. The priests didn't simply do this as an empty ritual but because they believed it was something that gave the living God pleasure.

As someone whom Jesus has made a 'priest', you, too, can bring pleasure to the living God by the sacrifice you bring to him, and what brings him most pleasure is when you lift up the person of Jesus.

This is an amazing calling! You are called to revel in the love of God which gave Jesus for you, the forgiveness and healing that flow from him and the grace that can pour through you to others. Thinking and acting on these things brings deep pleasure to God, and will bring a sense of fulfilment to you as you step into the shoes he created for you. Be his priest and bring him pleasure.

Praise God

"Praise the LORD..."

Psalm 148.1

All creation is called to praise God in this psalm – everyone and everything, living and inanimate, and this includes us.

Our personal challenge is that we are called to praise God. You might think you are reasonably obedient to this call because you try to praise him at some point each day and certainly enter into corporate times of worship at church. However, the call to praise is more than this; it involves every part of you.

Praising God for the happy and grateful parts of yourself seems natural, but what about the other parts of you that might be frustrated, hurting and disappointed? According to Psalm 103.1, these parts of you are called to praise as well: 'all my inmost being, praise his holy name.'

See yourself before the throne of God, bringing your joy and thanks to him, but also your disappointments, frustrations and hurts, and remember that he reigns over all things.

God's promises

Now the LORD was gracious to Sarah as he had said, and the LORD did for Sarah what he had promised.

Genesis 21.1

The Lord's faithfulness to Sarah, the wife of Abraham, is summarised in this verse. It says everything he had promised her came about, and as Sarah looked back on her life, no doubt she would have said a big 'Amen' to this verse and told everyone how true it was – as indeed we can see for ourselves as we look back over her story in Genesis. However, what we are not reminded of is that Sarah did not always perceive God's faithfulness as events unfolded! She laughed in disbelief when she was first told that God was going to use her to bear a child (Genesis 18.12), but as she looked back at the end of her life, she would have laughed with joy and wonder.

Holding on to the faithfulness of God is hard, and perhaps the only way to do this is to glimpse him as a person. The promises of God are not mantras for endless repetition, but the utterances of the living person of God. When we ponder his love, it is all about the attitude of the living God towards us, and not simply a comforting feeling. The more you can commit to a relationship with the living God, the more his promises and his love will mean to you. Perhaps there is a particular promise you are holding on to at the moment? Try to 'hear' the promise coming from the lips of Jesus to you.

It's OK to wallow

There is an encouraging gem for us in this 'woe to you' passage. Jesus is warning against being so hung up on the smaller matters of faith that the bigger picture gets lost. A huge part of the bigger picture is the love of God and Jesus says it is utterly wrong to neglect his love.

> "Woe to you Pharisees, because you give God a tenth of your mint, rue and all other kinds of garden herbs, but you neglect justice and the love of God. You should have practised the latter without leaving the former undone."
>
> **Luke 11.42**

Yet so many of us do exactly this. We bypass it, forget about it and don't remember to find it afresh. The consequence is that we get waylaid by secondary matters and lose the ability to pass on his love to others.

Spending time wallowing in God's love can seem self-indulgent when we sense there are weightier matters needing our prayer. However, Jesus calls us back to what is perhaps the greatest calling: to rest and abide in his love so that it flows out to others. Right now, turn your attention to his love for you and rest in it.

Qualified to serve

' How much more, then, will the blood of Christ...cleanse our consciences... so that we may serve the living God!'

Hebrews 9.14

What stops you serving God? It might be that you sense something in your past is keeping you from being used by God and you feel disqualified because of what you have done. This verse cuts right to the heart of the matter. The writer to the Hebrews says that the very act of Jesus dying for you takes away your sin and also has the power to cleanse your conscience, so you can be utterly free to serve God.

We all know the 'facts' of the cross and are probably aware of having been forgiven. However, our consciences tell us a different story because we may not actually *feel* forgiven. If this is the case, you need to come back to the truth proclaimed in this verse, that you have been washed clean and are free to serve God. You may know you are forgiven, but maybe you need to ask the Holy Spirit to cleanse your conscience so you can live in the truth of the cross.

The more the light of this truth touches you, the more you can bask in it and start to believe you can do good to other people without listening to your inner voice asking, "Just what do you think you are doing?" You can pray without fearing that your prayers are a joke! There is nothing that disqualifies you; because of Jesus, you are totally qualified to serve God.

God the rock

You have forgotten God your Saviour; you have not remembered the Rock, your fortress.

Isaiah 17.10

This simple fact – that when we most need to remember the presence of God and all this brings to us, we forget it – is the cause of so many of our worries and anxieties.

However, if you have spent time being aware of God's presence when you were not in a crisis, you are more likely to remember it in a moment of need. In other words, taking time each day to find an awareness of God's presence with you is going to sow something into your life, and it will become far more natural for you to return to him at different times of the day.

Speak these words slowly to God, words that are based on today's verse: "O my Rock, my fortress." As you speak, explore the words in your mind. What does it mean for you today that God is your rock and your fortress? Hopefully these words will become engrained within you, so when you need them throughout the day they will come back to you.

> 66 *I am going to send you what my Father has promised* 99
>
> **Luke 24.49**

Changing the world

Here, Luke recalls one of the final promises of Jesus, that even though he was going to ascend to heaven he would send the gift of the Holy Spirit to his disciples. This Spirit would be the very indwelling presence and power of Jesus for them. Jesus' promise hasn't changed over the years so the question is, do you believe in the availability of this power and presence for your life?

As you ponder the hours ahead of you, perhaps mentally going through all the various activities and events of which you will be a part, you either go through these times being pushed and shaped by them, or you see yourself as someone profoundly affected by the Holy Spirit whom Jesus has sent. Paul uses the beautiful phrase that 'your body is a temple of the Holy Spirit' (1 Corinthians 6.19). In other words, and daunting as it may seem, you are going to change every situation in which you find yourself because you are carrying this profound presence and power of the Holy Spirit.

Take a few moments to think through the hours ahead and see yourself not simply in your weakness, but rather as a carrier of the Holy Spirit.

Why not me?

Jesus describes the act of healing as setting someone free in this story. Although the leader of the synagogue encouraged people not to seek healing on the Sabbath, Jesus opposed him, implying that every day is a day for God to bring freedom. Jesus came to bring freedom and took a firm stand for it.

> '...a woman was there who had been crippled by a spirit for eighteen years. She was bent over and could not straighten up at all. When Jesus saw her, he called her forward and said to her, "Woman, you are set free from your infirmity."'
> **Luke 13.11–12**

So what would Jesus love to bring to your life? We can get so used to our wounds, burdens and sicknesses that it never occurs to us to seek freedom from them.

As Jesus looks at your life, what would he make of the things you carry around with you? What is it that stops you bringing these things to him? It may be a lack of conviction that he wants to do anything about them, fear in case nothing happens or perhaps you simply do not know what to do?

Whatever you feel, a good place to begin is to read the Gospel stories of Jesus healing people and think about this question, 'Why wouldn't it happen to me?'

> '...and there before me was a throne...'
>
> **Revelation 4.2**

Standing before the throne of God

The Bible speaks of both Isaiah and John having visions of the throne of God. What was happening as they had their visions? Did God specifically arrange the angels in the right place so the 'snapshot' received by Isaiah and John was just right? Actually, what happened was that for a moment in their lives their eyes were opened so they could see what was there all the time, hidden from human sight yet real none the less. You may never see a vision of the throne of God, but you do live in its presence on a daily basis. Jesus is king; he reigns and his throne is a reality.

If you could actually see the throne of God in the sky above you all day, what difference would it make? Surely it would change your day completely! The presence of God would not be something to hold on to by faith, because it would be staring you in the face. Prayer would be entirely natural as you looked up and saw God's power. Temptation would probably lose its grip over you in the light of his awesome presence with you.

You can't see it, but the throne of God really is there, so tune into this reality and live it.

Bible-based praise

> *And they sang a new song before the throne*
>
> **Revelation 14.3**

Praying according to how we are feeling at a particular time is natural, yet if our prayer lives are governed by our feelings or what is on our minds, the danger is that if we do not feel like worshipping then we won't.

Set patterns of prayer can be so helpful in avoiding this tendency, although there is a danger that we lose spontaneity and creativity in our relationship with God. However you 'organise' your prayers, there is a calling to sing a new song to God – not literally, but certainly to ensure your praise and worship is not simply the same as it was yesterday and the day before.

Prayer linked to Bible readings can be helpful. What is it from your daily reading of the Bible that you can use to 'feed' your worship? What aspect of God's character does a particular passage highlight and which you can turn into worship? Is there a verse you can use as a prayer of praise to God?

Your relationship with God is kept alive and fresh by singing a new song to him every day.

Forgiveness

> **"** *I, even I, am he who blots out your transgressions, for my own sake, and remembers your sins no more.* **"**
>
> **Isaiah 43.25**

Why do we hold on to memories of what we have done wrong if it's true that God blots out our sins and remembers them no more?

One of the reasons for this is that we have not yet fully grasped that the way God deals with sin is by paying for it. He puts the punishment for it on Jesus and doesn't simply pretend it never happened. Yet when we continue to dwell on our sins, it is as if they are still constantly present with us, even though the truth is that they have been dealt with, fully paid for and we actually do not have the right to keep dwelling on them.

Is there something from your past that still weighs upon you, even though you have confessed it many times already? Jesus did not take it from you so that you and he could both have it. He took it from you so that you would be free. Grasping this truth begins with worship. Worship Jesus for what he has already done with your sin; don't ask him to take it away any more, but worship him that he already has.

As sure as the day is day

❝*This is what the LORD says: 'If you can break my covenant with the day and my covenant with the night, so that day and night no longer come at their appointed time, then... David will no longer have a descendant to reign on his throne.'*❞

Jeremiah 33.20–21

There is so much hope and promise in this verse. Our faith is that the descendant of David who reigns on the throne is Jesus, and as long as it is light during the day and dark during the night, Jesus is still King.

Sometimes we need to be reminded of this. We all have times in our lives when it seems that we are in the hands of powers and forces beyond our control, but the truth is that Jesus is still King; he is still sovereign and reigning over all. Faith is holding on to the truth of what we believe when all around us circumstances are screaming the opposite.

There is an amazing moment in John 11.27, when Jesus and Martha are standing before the tomb of her brother Lazarus. Martha is confused and hurt, and yet she is able to say to Jesus, "I believe that you are the Christ, the Son of God, who was to come into the world." Despite the circumstances, she held on to her faith.

If things are tough for you today, remind yourself that Jesus is still Lord and reigning over all, and say – even through gritted teeth – "I believe you are King today."

True friendship

At the end of the story of Gideon, after all his service to his people, we are told that the people turned away from God and didn't show kindness to Gideon's family.

The same word that is translated as 'kindness' in this verse is one of the words God used to reveal his character in Exodus 34.6, which says that he is 'abounding in love'. The point is this: people may indeed fail you, they probably always will, but the promise of God is that he offers you a friendship that can never be bettered, and he will never let you down.

There are three implications of this:

First, you can keep coming back to God. No matter what you do wrong, or how many times you feel you have failed, you can keep coming back to God, who will never close the door to you.

Secondly, you can share your concerns with honesty and trust. God is not going to be shocked by anything you share with him. He has been dealing with humanity for quite a while now and has probably heard everything!

Thirdly, you can trust him. His infinite love and patience means he will always be there for you.

The kindness of God is real; you can take it to heart and be assured of it. He is with you now, wanting to be closer than anyone else is to you. Trust in this kindness and begin to talk to him.

At peace with who you are

'A heart at peace gives life to the body, but envy rots the bones.'

Proverbs 14.30

Two opposing states of mind are noted in today's verse: a peace with who we are and what we have, contrasted with an envy because we want more or want what others may have.

A heart at peace stems from being at peace with who you are: a unique creation of God, redeemed by Jesus in order that you might be more of the person he made you to be. You might sometimes want to be different – and might even think that God would like you to be someone else – but far from bringing him pleasure, this would sadden him beyond measure, as a unique part of his creation would be lost to the world.

Being who you are brings glory to God, as each of us reflects something unique about him. However, it may be that we only begin to reflect him when we start to believe this and give thanks for it. As you go through this day, the people you meet will find something in you which they cannot find in anyone else. You are God's gift to those you will meet today.

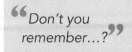

Reflecting on our prayers

The disciples were in the boat and wondering where their lunch was coming from! In his encouragement to keep their faith alive, Jesus referred them back to the two episodes where the 5,000 and 4,000 people had been fed, and then went on to ask his disciples this question, "Don't you remember...?"

When we pray to God and he answers our prayers, this shouldn't be the end of the matter. We should learn from prayer so that we are led closer to God and have our faith built up for the future.

It's worth thinking back over the past week and considering what God has done for you. Which prayers has he answered? What you have learnt from these occasions – about God, his character, goodness and provision? A further step in this reflection is to decide what you will take into the days and weeks ahead. If God has done something for you and you have learned from it, what difference will it make in the future?

God's desire is for relationship with you and not simply to be an eternal slot machine. He has done all he can do to foster that relationship, and what counts now is how you respond to him.

Practice makes perfect!

'*About midnight Paul and Silas were praying and singing hymns to God*'

Acts 16.25

Surely this is the sort of thing Christians should be doing? At first sight there is nothing unusual about this statement, but the reality is that Paul and Silas were in prison. Added to this, the reason they were imprisoned was because they had been obedient to God. They had gone to a specific area and during their time there had delivered a girl from the influence of the devil. This had landed them in prison, and to some extent they must have wondered why it had all turned out that way; they had been obedient and look where it had landed them!

You may not be able to identify with them in their physical situation, but you can probably understand their likely confusion. The lesson to be learned from Paul and Silas is the importance of turning to God in prayer and praise rather than wallowing in confusion and doubt.

However, this is far easier said than done, and unless your natural inclination is to turn to God when you have moments of crisis, it probably won't happen. Think about some small event in your life that is a source of confusion or worry, and use this to practise turning your attention away from the problem and onto God. The more you can do it with small issues, the more natural it will be when more major issues come along.

It's God's opinion that counts

> *Jesus straightened up and asked her, "Woman, where are they? Has no-one condemned you?" "No-one, sir," she said. "Then neither do I condemn you," Jesus declared.*
> **John 8.10**

These remain some of the most powerful and releasing words spoken by Jesus. Within a short space of time, this woman had moved from a position of being vilified, accused and condemned, to being pronounced innocent and free. The liberating implication of these words is that if Jesus does not condemn us, the opinions of others is of little regard.

Catching God's opinion of us is vital, yet so many people still live under the impression that God himself is against them, following them around to record all their failings. Paul addressed this in his letter to the Romans, when he asked, 'Who will bring any charge against those whom God has chosen?' (Romans 8.33). It is a question we too would do well to ponder. He then went on to declare it could not be God who was against his chosen ones, because he had sent Jesus for them. You are chosen by God and Jesus cannot be against you, since he gave up his life for you.

If you can believe this, you can lift your head up high, for if God himself looks at you without condemnation then why are you afraid of the opinion of others? God looks at you with love and is totally for you.

Trust

> 'He provides food for the cattle and for the young ravens when they call.'
>
> **Psalm 147.9**

Surely this psalm isn't saying that we are meant to simply sit and wait for God to provide us with food? What it does say is that if God's care extends to animals and what may seem the most insignificant part of creation, how much more does he care for us? It is not so much a call to sit still and wait for God to put the food into our mouths, but rather a call to trust in the extent of his care for us and that care includes providing for us.

You may be facing difficulties in your life. If so, ask yourself what is the level of your trust in God? What is it you actually trust God to do for you today? If you are honest, most of the time you probably expect to get through the day largely by your own efforts and skills. You would like God to continue keeping you alive by his sustaining power, but you would also like to think that you can get through the day without being too dependent on him.

Start to grow your trust in him by choosing one thing you need today that only God can give. It may be an inner attitude. There are plenty of things within you that only God can do, such as a changed attitude to someone or more patience to face a frustrating situation. Whatever it might be, find strength in some words from Psalm 13.5, 'I trust in your unfailing love', and bring your specific need into a place of trust.

> ❛...worship the LORD in the splendour of his holiness.❜
>
> **1 Chronicles 16.29**

Holiness

Holiness can have quite a negative feel to it! It can imply giving up everything you think of as fun, going around with a long face while pretending to be full of joy or cutting yourself off from anything in the world that might possibly contaminate you.

The most holy person must have been Jesus, the Son of God. Yet we read of him eating and drinking, mixing with all sorts of people and going to parties where he presumably didn't spend the whole time condemning everyone or he would not have received many return invitations! What does this say about holiness?

Holiness is more to do with what you embrace than what you give up. It is about embracing the depth of the Father's love for you, the presence of Jesus with you as you pray and living as one who bears his name and his Spirit wherever you go. This is a holiness that brings joy to others; it is attractive and reflects the wonder of the person of Jesus.

Take a moment to specifically embrace these truths so that they will be with you throughout the day.

His glory is here

> *And they were calling to one another: "Holy, holy, holy is the LORD Almighty; the whole earth is full of his glory."*
>
> **Isaiah 6.3**

This verse formed part of Isaiah's vision of heaven that was to completely change his life. In his vision, he was granted a glimpse of what the angels saw, which was the earth full of God's glory. Note that it was not a case of the earth being full of God's glory one day when things improved, but it is full of his glory now.

Perhaps what the angels see is the all-pervading presence of God throughout creation and among those he has created. All too often what we see is gloom, hopelessness and the fears caused by the situations facing us, yet the angels see glory!

If you could see the light you bear, and the light that every believer around you bears, maybe you, too, would be able to glimpse the wonder of the earth being full of the glory of God.

Catch the reality of the light within you by taking these words from Jeremiah 15.16 and saying them to yourself for two or three minutes: "I bear your name, O LORD God Almighty." Focus on the truth of them and begin to sense something of the glory that is in you and which you take with you wherever you go.

It's your right

Yet to all who received him, to those who believed in his name, he gave the right to become children of God

John 1.12

Calling God 'Father' is nice and comforting, but it carries with it far more than this. It is about the right to be in a unique relationship and to enjoy all the privileges that come with it. This relationship is permanent; no matter what you do, you can never stop being your father's child.

'Father' is not a random word you might suddenly decide to use one day. Actually you have permission, 'the right', to call God 'Father' not because you want to, but because he decrees it. It does not depend on whether or not you feel like it, or whether you have been good enough for it; God has done this.

As you look forward to the day ahead, you bear God's name. You have his permission and the right, given to you by God himself, to forget what may have gone before and to face this day as a child of the Father, knowing you are loved by him and that his character dwells within you so you can draw upon it at any time.

The faithfulness of God

> '...if we are faithless, he will remain faithful, for he cannot disown himself.'
>
> **2 Timothy 2.13**

If someone fails us or lets us down somehow, it is natural for us to cool a little towards them. Our treatment of others often mirrors their treatment of us. And we can be so quick to judge God by our own standards.

This verse proclaims that God is quite different. Whereas we may fail him, let him down and often forget him completely, Paul says God will never do this to us. Indeed, it is impossible for God to treat us like this, as faithfulness is in his very nature.

You might feel that God has let you go because of what you have done. It is easy to assume your past actions or present attitudes have caused him to change his plans and dreams for you. Yet what if this is simply not true and the change has been on your part rather than his? Perhaps he has never moved away? If this is true, then all it takes is for you to trust again in his wonderful love for you and step back into his presence.

Whatever you may be like, God is, and always will be, utterly faithful to you. Let these words fill your mind now.

Looking at his love

Whenever we turn to God in prayer, there is often an initial anxiety as we wonder what God thinks of us. Knowing everything about us, what will he think of our prayer? Often the mental image of a stern God judging our words needs to be laid aside.

These words from Psalm 145 are words that are scattered throughout the Bible – a constant reminder to us of who God really is and what his heart towards us is like. They are words we would do well to call to mind every time we come to him in prayer.

God's nature, and his choice, is to be gracious and compassionate. In other words, God acts from his heart rather than according to what we may or may not deserve. Anger rises slowly within him, not as a quick reaction to our failings, and he is rich in love, which flows generously from him to us.

These lovely words can be made into a personal prayer through which you can enter into his presence daily: 'Father you are...Jesus you are....Holy Spirit you are.... gracious and compassionate, slow to anger and rich in love.'

It goes on and on and on...

When Mary was told she was going to become the mother of Jesus, she was given this amazing promise. It is a promise which has been unfolding from that day until now, and will continue to be a promise we can trust every day for the rest of our lives.

The promise is quite simply that the kingdom of God will never end. It grew during the ministry of Jesus, continued to grow after his Ascension, expanded through the ministry of the Apostles and has carried on growing through every Christian ever since.

The kingdom of God will grow some more today in and through your life. Whatever you are planning to do, God will be acting in your life, seeking to transform you a little bit more into his likeness.

He is also working through you. You are his hands and his mouth to bring the extension of his kingdom to those around you. Every person with whom you come into contact is someone God wants to experience his kingdom; it may even be as simple as passing on a word of encouragement. It may not seem much for you, but it might be the only touch of kindness some people receive in the whole day.

> **"**...do not be negligent now, for the LORD has chosen you to stand before him and serve him**"**
> **2 Chronicles 29.11**

Staying in his presence

One of the tensions we often face in our Christian lives is working out what we are meant to do and what we should leave for God to do. This verse provides a little insight into where to begin. It starts with vision.

The calling to all Christians is "do not be negligent" about who you are. In other words, you need to be attentive to the fact that you have been chosen to be in God's presence and serve him. Your ability to see yourself as being chosen by him will govern what acts of service flow from you.

It is very easy to neglect this command and think of yourself as a failure compared to other people. In fact, it is often easier to think like this than to see yourself as God sees you, a person chosen to stand in his presence. What's more, you are not just given permission to see yourself standing in his presence, but are actually commanded to do so.

Take a moment right now to consider this truth: wherever you are physically, you are also 'before him', actually in his presence. Let this truth run through your mind: 'I stand before you Lord.'

Saying thank you

Hannah had been crying out to the Lord for a child, and when her request was answered, the Bible records a beautiful prayer of praise and thanksgiving to God. She doesn't simply thank God for answering her specific prayer, but allows her thanksgiving to lead into praise for the whole character of God.

Luke 17.11–19 records the story of the ten lepers who were healed, and the one who came back to give thanks. We may be quite obedient in following the command to cast our burdens onto Jesus (1 Peter 5.7), but how good are we at coming back in thanksgiving?

It is a good discipline to spend some time each day before the Lord, reviewing the past 24 hours. What things have gone well and where have you seen his hand at work? Can you recall specific answers to prayer? Also consider which things have not gone so well and whether there are things for which you are sorry.

It is so easy to cry out to see more of God at work in your life, but by letting the days pass you by without any real reflection or times of thanksgiving is to miss out on seeing the many miracles and loving touches that God performs in your life.

The words we use

> *'The mouth of the righteous is a fountain of life'*

Proverbs 10.11

When we talk to people, especially if they are in particular need, we want to say the right thing and avoid putting our foot in it and making things worse! Sometimes it can be quite a struggle to think of the right words to say. However, this verse says we don't have to try too hard.

You are one of the righteous, and therefore your mouth is a fountain of life to those you meet. This has nothing to do with your own ability, but is all down to the simple fact that you have the Spirit of God living within you. You need to remember to tune into the one who is living within you, rather than try too hard to say the right thing. It is not about what you can say to people, but what would Jesus say to them?

When you are next in conversation with someone, keep the word 'Jesus' in your mind as a question. What you are really asking is, "Jesus, what would you say to this person?" This is different from trying to come up with some wise words to share, because instead you are looking to the source of living water flowing out of you. If something comes to mind, gently share it. You don't have to say this is what Jesus says, as there is always the possibility you may be wrong, but the words you speak might be exactly what that person needs to hear. You are a fountain of life – so at least give the living water a chance to flow!

A gift to us | 1

"This, then, is how you should pray"

Matthew 6.9

The prayer we know as the Lord's Prayer is strange in some ways. It is a prayer given to us by Jesus, which has become a set prayer we recite line by line in churches everywhere. It was actually given as a reaction to those who babbled words without thinking about them, and Jesus is probably horrified to see his guidance has become just the same – words often spoken at speed without undue thought.

A meaningful way of praying the Lord's Prayer is to take it phrase by phrase, spending some minutes repeating each phrase and praying through the sense of it, rather than simply repeating the words. As you ponder each phrase in turn, ask yourself some questions: what do the words stir up in you on this particular occasion? What does the phrase prompt you to pray? It is worth paying special attention to those parts of the prayer you would rather skip over.

This prayer is Jesus' gift to you; it presumably reflects the things on his heart as he talked to his Father. He gave it to you out of love, so that you might enjoy the wonder of the relationship that is fed by prayer.

> **"** *Our Father in heaven* **"**
> **Matthew 6.9**

Come as a child | 2

It is interesting to listen to prayers and note who is being addressed in them. Most people speak to 'Lord', presumably on the understanding that this covers all options! However, Jesus encouraged us to talk to our 'Father'. It isn't a matter of your prayer becoming invalid if you don't speak to the right person, but instead is an invitation to share in the same relationship with God that Jesus himself enjoyed. It was his great delight to call God 'Father', and his longing is for you to enter into that relationship as well.

Some people prefer to pray to Jesus because the very word 'father' reminds them of negative images, perhaps caused by an unhappy childhood or an abusive father-child relationship. However, it is important not to create an image of Father God from earthly memories or ideas. Earthly fathers may well be far less than perfect, but this does not mean our Father God is the same.

Out of his incredible love for you, and his desire that you should have a real sense of your heavenly father, Jesus gave himself so he could reflect the wonder of God's fatherhood. He himself said: "Anyone who has seen me has seen the Father" (John 14.9). At the end of his ministry, Jesus was able to say to his Father: "I have made you known..." (John 17.26). If there is any doubt in your mind about the nature of God the Father, his kindness or what he wants for you, look at Jesus.

Take time to whisper the word 'Father', and as you do so, let it begin to express something of the way God sees you as his child.

It's all about character | 3

" …hallowed be your name "
Matthew 6.9

The literal meaning of this phrase is something like, "may your name be held holy", but what does it really mean? The name of God does not simply refer to what he is called, but instead refers to everything that belongs to him; it is about his character.

In this verse, it is the name of the Father that is holy. In other words, it is the character of the Father that we must not forget to take seriously. Do we tend to neglect taking his character seriously? Sadly, we are probably guilty of this quite often – and it is always to our disadvantage!

On every occasion when we forget the Father's love for us, it bothers him. This is an astounding thought, and Jesus revealed something of the Father's desperation that we really grasp and do not forget his love. So many people view the love of God as distant, or even worse as something warped, believing that although he says he loves us he is actually behind all manner of hurtful and arbitrary acts of unkindness to us.

We will never hope to understand why evil things happen, but one of the first things Jesus encouraged in the prayer he gave is this: never be tempted to lose sight of the truth and the reality that you are uniquely and individually loved by Father God. Spend a few moments now to accept the wonder of his love for you.

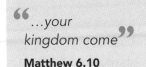

The kingdom without limit | 4

For those of us who live under a monarchy, the kingdom of which we are a part has geographical limits. When we physically go beyond these limits, the laws and ways of our kingdom cease to apply to us. The kingdom of God is different, it has no geographical borders. Instead it is the Father's kingdom that surrounds Jesus. On every occasion the presence of Jesus is with us, the kingdom is surrounding him and there is no limit to what it brings.

In the Gospels, everything Jesus did was a part of his Father's kingdom. Jesus has been made Lord of all, the one who reigns over all and who has everything under his feet. When you invite him to come close, you invite his rule, his reign and his power as well.

Instead of launching straight into prayer, try to find an awareness of the reality of the presence of Jesus and the Father's kingdom. Then anything might happen!

Being in agreement | 5

" ...your will be done... "

Matthew 6.10

Many people tend to end their prayers with something like, "Not my will, but yours be done." It does sound submissive and holy, and it also comes from the mouth of Jesus as he prayed in the Garden of Gethsemane, but is it always an appropriate prayer? Since the whole of our lives are in submission to the Father, in this general sense it is an appropriate prayer. Yet praying along these lines can divert us from the fact that the Father has already revealed his will, and his desire is we catch it and bring it into being.

God has revealed his will through Jesus, who says he came to bring abundant life. This is not something Jesus decided to do for us; he came to do the Father's will. Similarly, it says in 1 John 3.8 that the reason Jesus appeared was to destroy the devil's work. Again, this was not something Jesus did on his own initiative; he came to do this because it was what the Father wanted.

When we ask for things in prayer, we are just not sure God wants to do them for us, and so we add a little prayer of submission in case he wants us to continue struggling on for a little while longer! We need to learn to pray this phrase of the Lord's Prayer with conviction, "your will be done!" In other words, we align ourselves to the things Jesus came to do and we submit to this happening in our lives.

Reflecting heaven | 6

This phrase more than any other opens up the incredible nature of God's desire for the world, and therefore also his desire for us who live in it.

There is probably no doubt in your mind that heaven (however you perceive it) reflects the wonder, the will and the beauty of God; what God wants surrounds him in heaven. His desire is for his will to be done on earth in the same way as it is in heaven so that the whole earth, and the life of each individual, will reflect the wonder, will and beauty of God.

Some human suffering genuinely seems to bring profound glory to God, but it is our lack of vision that says it is the only way God can be glorified. Rather than endorsing suffering, the fact that God can work through something that does not reflect the wonder of heaven shows something amazing about the power of God.

God's desire is for the glory of heaven to be reflected on this earth. As you pray for events in your life and in the lives of others, begin by catching the vision of how these situations would look through the perspective of heaven and then reflect this in your prayers.

Our generous father | 7

❝ *Give us today our daily bread.* ❞

Matthew 6.11

Behind this verse is the recognition that ultimately everything we have comes from the hand of the Father who provides for us. Asking God for the things we need, even when we have the resources to buy without his divine intervention, underlines this truth for us.

We need to learn to ask with the expectation that God will give. He has just invited us to pray for the coming of his kingdom, so it is unlikely he will want to give us one thing and yet be unwilling to give us others. In Luke's account of the parable of the talents (Luke 19.11–27), the biggest judgment was reserved for the man who felt God was mean. When we are told to ask for our daily bread, this encouragement comes from the one who gave us the most valuable thing he could, Jesus. Indeed Paul writes in Romans 8.32, 'He who did not spare his own Son, but gave him up for us all – how will he not also, along with him, graciously give us all things?'

This is the God who invites us to bring our requests to him, who has given us Jesus out of his love for us, and who longs for us to trust in our Father God.

Passing on forgiveness | 8

"Forgive us our debts, as we also have forgiven our debtors."

Matthew 6.12

Traditionally, we use the word 'trespass' or 'sin' when we pray this prayer, but the word 'debt' is probably a closer translation of the original, which carries the sense of 'something owed.' The difficulty is that we can appreciate the first part of the phrase, but may be less keen on the second!

We are encouraged to be honest about the way we approach God, and to face up to how we can ask for God's forgiveness when we do wrong, but what if we are not willing to be just as forgiving to those who have hurt us? It is not a matter of forgiving others in order to earn our own forgiveness, but about eradicating unforgiveness from our hearts by receiving forgiveness from God and then passing it on to others.

If you know someone who has hurt you, begin by rejoicing in the total forgiveness God has given you through Jesus, and then ask for the grace to pass this same forgiveness on to them.

God encourages you to forgive, even though it can be so tough, because he knows this is what will give you a level of peace that little else can achieve.

Being honest | 9

And lead us not into temptation

Matthew 6.13

We are all aware of the main things in life which are constant temptations to us; the areas in which we battle. This remarkable phrase invites us to be utterly honest with ourselves and with the God who loves us about who we are and our weaknesses.

This prayer invites us to acknowledge the truth that it is not God who takes us into these places of temptation, but that we are drawn there either by ourselves or by other forces at work. Yet despite this, these are still areas about which the Father longs for our honesty.

Dare you trust that his love for you is so great that he will not cast you out if you disclose to him the areas in your life which cause you most struggle? Deep down, you may well be thinking God will be so shocked by what you reveal that he will run away in complete surprise at what you are like. We all need to remember he probably knows what we are really like already!

The extent of your friendship and fellowship with God is determined by whether you can share your weaknesses with him in the trust that he will not punish you, but instead will actually love you even more (if that is possible) because of the honesty and closeness you are revealing. What do you want to bring to him right now?

> **"** ...but deliver
> us from the
> evil one.**"**
> **Matthew 6.13**

When willpower is not enough | 10

This final phrase in the Lord's Prayer acknowledges our total dependence upon God; it recognises that we are not able to deliver ourselves from evil but need the constant help and intervention of God.

The Bible does speak of the battle in which God is involved against the devil, a battle in which we, too, are included. It can be easy to look at events or at other people and see how their lives or situations have been influenced by forces opposed to God, but it can be far harder to face up bravely to where the devil has his foothold and activity in our own life.

What can you do about this? It is very tempting to try using willpower or self-control to break out from negative influences upon you, but this phrase of the prayer reveals that willpower is often not the solution; you need the intervention of God.

A common prayer in some parts of the church is the very simple phrase, 'Lord Jesus Christ, have mercy on me.' This can be used on all manner of occasions, and certainly when you need his help. It acknowledges your need of Jesus and invites him to step into your life with the mercy that brought him into this world in the first place. It is a form of shorthand for saying, "Jesus, there are things going on over which I have no control, things that seek to pull me away from you. Step into my life with your inexhaustible mercy, and bring the change that only you can."

Going over the top

'Glory in his holy name'

1 Chronicles 16.10

As an English phrase, this doesn't really mean much. However, the original Hebrew word, which is translated 'glory', carries a number of nuances to its meaning, including a sense of acting wildly or madly and even going over the top with excitement!

Why would we do this? The reason is because what we are talking about is such good news it deserves a reaction. We are glorying in God's name, his character. The Lord God of heaven and earth, the creator of everything, loves us uniquely and wonderfully. This is the cause for our rejoicing: it was worth rejoicing in yesterday, is worth it today and will be worth it tomorrow, because this good news is equally true today as when it was first heard. Its relevance and power has not changed simply because we think we know it well. In fact, when it comes to pondering the love of God, the old saying is probably true: familiarity breeds contempt.

Right now, take a moment to think about who God is for you. What does it mean to you that he is with you and he loves you? Memorise this verse and come back to it from time to time. Each time you do, consciously rejoice in something wonderful about the God who loves you.

God's view of us

Trust in the LORD with all your heart and lean not on your own understanding

Proverbs 3.5

This verse sounds like good advice, but the problem is that we frequently ignore it, especially when it comes down to thinking about who we are. We make judgments based on a variety of things: our feelings, our past and what we perceive other people are thinking about us. Yet our calling is to trust in the Lord, to believe what the Bible says God thinks about us and to trust in his love.

Sometimes this can seem very difficult, because our negative feelings about ourselves are screaming at us, and we simply do not feel the trust we are called to have. Perhaps this is why it is trust – because we are being asked to believe in something we do not feel. If we felt it, then we would not have to show trust.

Trust is sometimes a matter of putting your hand out in the darkness and believing God is holding it, whether or not you have any awareness of it.

To trust in his love for you is not a matter of indulgence, it is a command.

The love of God

'Keep yourselves in God's love...'

Jude 21

The challenge in this verse is also encouraging: Jude is telling us never to lose sight of the fact that God loves us. What a wonderful command – to always believe I am loved by God! However much we dwell on the love of God, we can never reach a point where God would say, "You've gone too far now, I don't love you that much!" What a wonderful way to start your day, and how encouraging to keep returning regularly to this remarkable truth that you are loved by God.

As a Christian, you have turned your face, in some way and in some measure, to God and responded to his love. So why not go further? There is nothing you can do to make him stop loving you, and also nothing you can do to make him love you more than he already does.

It sounds very self-indulgent to ponder this truth, but actually it is being obedient! Take a few moments right now to rest in the wonderful love God has for you.

Magnifying God

It really is an act of faith and trust to be able to stand before God and call on his help, 'for his name's sake'. All too often we make everything about ourselves: do I deserve his help? How much do I sense his love? The truth is, it is all about him.

Throughout the Bible, God reveals himself as a gracious and compassionate God, slow to anger and abounding in love. This is how he wants to be known, and how he wants to be at the forefront of your mind as you approach him, trusting in who he is and not in yourself.

This can sound so easy, but in practice it is hard to turn away from feelings. Before you pray, spend a few minutes focused not on yourself or your particular needs, but upon God, his love for you and the wonder of his power. In times of prayer, something tends to be magnified, and it is far better that this is God rather than your problems.

Knowing Jesus

'What is more, I consider everything a loss compared to the surpassing greatness of knowing Christ Jesus my Lord'

Philippians 3.8

This is quite some statement. There is nothing in life that compares to knowing Jesus, and what's more, it is so wonderful to know him that everything else just gets in the way.

If you are honest, you may not be able to say this verse with the same conviction as Paul. Many people enjoy their relationship with Christ, but there are other things they enjoy as well, and as wonderful as your fellowship with him might be, you can be made to feel a little guilty if other things rate highly in your enjoyment of life.

What this verse gives us is an amazing assurance that there is more. Knowing Jesus Christ can be the most exciting and wonderful thing in your life. Even if it is not so now, it can be. Jesus is not seeking to take everything from you because he is a spoilsport, he is seeking to get across to you the amazing fact that knowing him is better than anything else you can experience in this life.

If you get pleasure from other things, enjoy them and be thankful, but also listen to Jesus whispering in your ear, "There is something even better, come closer!"

Hard times

'After all that
Hezekiah had so
faithfully done,
Sennacherib king of
Assyria came and
invaded Judah.'

2 Chronicles 32.1

King Hezekiah was doing so well: he was being faithful and he really did lead his people back to God. We are told that in everything he did, he was careful to seek God (2 Chronicles 31.21). Yet in spite of all his faithfulness and goodness, something terrible happened and the country was invaded. He probably thought, "Why? Why, after all I have done, would God allow this to happen?"

Perhaps there are times when you might be tempted to think along these lines. You try to lead a good life and stay close to God, and then out of the blue something happens and quite naturally you ask, "Why should this happen to me?"

There is no answer to these questions, but what comes through the story of the invasion is something of Hezekiah's steadfastness and faith, and eventually the invading army was annihilated by God.

Things can happen to you that are probably inexplicable from a human perspective, often leaving you confused and hurt. However, the point is this: do not assume that because you are going through hard times God must be displeased with you, or you must have wandered away from him. What is certain is that he is not finished yet and there is more he wants to do.

Responding to the kindness of God

'But Hezekiah's heart was proud and he did not respond to the kindness shown him'

2 Chronicles 32.25

In yesterday's verse, we heard that Hezekiah was in many ways an amazing king who brought his people back to the worship of the living God. Yet in this last passage about his life, we are told that he went so wrong. His wrongdoing was not about any moral failure or political treachery, but simply that he stopped responding to God's kindness to him.

We are all probably just as guilty of overlooking God's kindness to us. It may be that you have been neglecting to thank him for his kindness, or are beginning to regard life's blessings as the results of your own efforts and goodness. Perhaps you realise you are walking down more legalistic paths, thinking that if you do 'this and that' then God will bless you, when all along God's goodness has been down to his kindness and not your behaviour.

The good news is that Hezekiah repented and turned back to God. It may be you also might need to turn back to God and once again start recognising that your blessings come from his wonderful kindness and responding to him with gratitude.

Finding his name

We would probably all say we have faith in God to help us, but the problem is when other people or pressures begin to have a hold on us. At moments like this, the tangible pressures surrounding us can seem more real than the help promised by God. We know God is strong, but sometimes it seems as though other things are stronger.

Jeremiah seeks to address this problem in this verse. The people are in the grip of captivity and God's help appears distant. Jeremiah's encouragement is to have faith. Even the words he uses are faith-building. Rather than speak directly of God, he refers to God as a 'Redeemer', a term which is directly relevant to their current struggles.

This is such a powerful encouragement to us. When you feel in need of particular help from God, bring his name to bear on what you need. In other words, call out to him as Provider if you are in need of provision or Healer if your need is for healing. What you are doing is putting your faith in the real person of God rather than in some vague notion that he might help you.

What can I do?

'The repairs next to him were made by the priests from the surrounding region.'

Nehemiah 3.22

When Nehemiah set about the task of rebuilding the walls of Jerusalem, each person or group of people was responsible for a particular section. No individual was responsible for everything, and all the people had their part to play.

We can all see there is much to be done in the world around us; the challenge is so great. However, God does not expect any individual to try to solve all the problems of the world single-handedly. Instead he gives a particular area of responsibility to each of us and helps us to make it our own challenge and calling.

There are many things you are called to do – things specifically assigned to you and no one else. If you took this responsibility seriously, you could have a real impact on those around you. One area is to guard what comes out of your mouth; James says the tongue can corrupt the whole body (James 3.6). If you regard life in terms of building the walls for God, perhaps the segment over which you can take responsibility is watching what comes out of your mouth. What a difference it would make to the people you are going to meet over the next few hours if you resolve not to say one negative thing. Perhaps it would begin to change your heart as well.

Finding his presence

66 *As for the foreigner...when he comes and prays towards this temple, then hear from heaven* 99

2 Chronicles 6.32

This verse is part of the prayer of dedication by Solomon for the newly built temple in Jerusalem. The essence of his prayer was that whatever went on in the lives of the people, both good and bad, they would face the temple, remember it is a place of the presence of God and turn back to the God who longed to save them. This longing is also relevant for us. Whatever is happening in your life, whether things are going well or quite the reverse, your calling is to come back to the knowledge of God's presence within you.

It is always tempting to launch straight into a time of prayer, especially if things seem desperate, but in his prayer Solomon urged the people to remember their calling to focus first on God's presence, and then allow the rest of their prayers to follow.

You are a temple of the Holy Spirit and his loving presence is within you. You do not have to summon God to come close to you since he is already with you. As you begin to pray, take a few minutes to recall the truth that he is in you. You bear his name and carry his presence. Let this truth bring peace to you as you begin to bring your concerns to God.

Small beginnings

The seventh time the servant reported, "A cloud as small as a man's hand is rising from the sea."

1 Kings 18.44

Elijah knew the rain was coming. Seven times Elijah sent his servant to see if the clouds were forming, and finally on the seventh trip the servant proclaimed that a small cloud could be seen. Perhaps panic was beginning to set in after the fourth or fifth trip to see the as yet nonexistent cloud! The point is that Elijah had been promised rain and he fully expected it to come. He watched out for it and rejoiced when he saw the beginning of the promise being fulfilled.

What issues are you praying about? Perhaps you have been praying about them for so long you are beginning to despair of getting any result. The encouragement from Elijah is to be expectant of an answer, and to watch for and rejoice in even the smallest of encouragements.

In this story it seems that the time between the appearance of the small cloud and the arrival of the storm was very short. So watch for the encouragements, delight in them and see them as the first fruits of God fulfilling his promises to you.

> *But it was because the LORD loved you...*

Deuteronomy 7.8

Changing your glasses

An old saying, 'Seeing the world through rose tinted spectacles' is about choosing to view life in a positive way. As Christians who bear God's presence, we, too, are called to view life with a specific outlook, with a vision of God's love.

In this part of Deuteronomy, Moses was reflecting upon the experiences of the Israelites and commenting that the reason for their success in battle was not because of their skills, but because of God's great love for them. Yet so often it is a real challenge for us to put on the spectacles of God's great love for us. The temptation is to think it is easier to remember God's love in times of blessing than in times of hardship, but in reality we are most likely to forget about him in times of blessing.

The ability to rest in the love of God at all times is something to cultivate. One way of doing this is to begin your prayers with the word 'Father' and then pause. Let the wonder of this word play through your mind, and along with it the knowledge that the one to whom you pray is also the Father of our Lord Jesus Christ. Begin your day with this one word, and let the knowledge of God's love for you grow.

The commitment of God

God has acted: he sent Jesus and this can never be reversed. What Jesus did in his life and ministry on earth can never be revoked; it stands for all time. Similarly, his death on the cross to take away our sins can never be reversed, so it must be true that there is nothing we cannot bring to him for forgiveness, and no sin he will not gladly bear so we might experience freedom.

The promise to bring abundant life was for all people throughout all ages, and when Jesus looks at you his dream and longing is for you to have abundant life. Therefore, there is no situation facing you that you cannot place into his hands.

The motive for all the actions of God is his overwhelming, inexhaustible love for his people. There is nothing you have done or could ever do that will cause his love for you to dry up. This is not a license to try God's patience, but an invitation to come again to his open arms. The love of God is there for you, and you can rest in it, revel in it and trust in it.

> 66 *Look, the Lamb of God, who takes away the sin of the world!* 99
> **John 1.29**

How can we improve?

John the Baptist made this declaration about Jesus, and it is still deeply challenging for us today. We all have an awareness of our sin; we do things, say things and think things we know are far from the ideal God has planned for us. Many times you have probably tried to improve, either by making resolutions or determining to be different next time, but this so often ends in disappointment at not doing better.

The glorious truth is that you are not meant to improve by yourself. Father God knew you would not be able to do this on your own and this is why he sent Jesus as the 'Lamb of God, who takes away the sins of the world.' You cannot do anything permanent about your life, but Jesus can. He has willingly paid the price for your sins, so you are utterly clean and guiltless before God. It is the Holy Spirit working within you who gives you the grace to walk away from those things and thoughts which pull you from God. It is not your strength, but his.

What is also astonishing is that God doesn't see you coming and think, "It's them again!" Rather, he delights that you are turning to him, wanting to draw on his forgiveness and grace. At times you would probably rather wallow in your mistakes and feel you have to atone for your sins yourself, or that you can only come back to God when you have made a real effort. Nothing could be further from God's heart; he is waiting with longing for you to come to him.

Free from the past

'Even though I was once a...'
1 Timothy 1.13

Paul is very honest about his past in his letter to Timothy. He describes himself as having been a blasphemer, a persecutor and a violent man. If you were equally honest about yourself, what would you say about your past? What were you once?

What is most surprising is that Paul says he was *once* like this; he no longer sees himself in this way. Paul had a real ability to put his past behind him and not allow himself to continue being plagued by it. So many of us could learn from this, as we all too often remain tied to our pasts, unable to break away from what has happened to us.

Freedom from the past has huge benefits for us. If you can walk away from your past, then you can walk into the future free from the guilt of what you have done. Not only does this bless you, it also honours the work of Jesus who sacrificed his life so you might know this freedom. Walking in it, rather than spurning or ignoring it, is a real sign of worship.

No one gives a gift and wants it to be ignored or thrown away. One of the gifts Jesus has given is a life free from your past and if you can declare, along with Paul, that you were once a sinner but now you are free, then the gift is received and the giver finds joy. What were you, and what are you now?

> *...for your law is my delight.*
>
> **Psalm 119.77**

Finding delight

When the psalmist declares these words, he is not just declaring that the commands themselves are so wonderful. Rather, he is proclaiming his love for the one behind the commandments, and his belief that his love is reciprocated. It is because of this that he knows the commands themselves flow from a heart of love, and he takes delight in them.

The Bible comes alive when we are able to sense the heart behind it. The pages were not written to rob us of fun, but to bring the delight of God to us. It all comes down to our trust in God's love. When we 'know and rely on the love God has for us' (1 John 4.16), we will begin to delight in his word, whereas until then it often seems to be a struggle and we can even resent the influence the Bible seeks to have upon us.

Whatever portion of the Bible you read today, bear in mind the reason he gave it to you was because he loves you. Then, as you catch this motive, allow yourself to delight in what you read.

Come and get me

> *'I have strayed like a lost sheep. Seek your servant'*
>
> **Psalm 119.176**

This honest and trusting statement is saying something like, 'I believe in you; I know you are there somewhere, but somehow I have wandered away. Please come and get me!'

There have probably been times when you could identify with what the writer of this psalm was saying. It is not that you have committed some horrendous sin or deliberately and consciously walked away from God, but somehow – like a sheep with his eyes fixed on the grass rather than the shepherd – you have wandered away and you are not quite sure where you are. In this situation, the best possible prayer is 'Seek your servant,' or to put it another way, 'Come and get me.'

The beauty of this prayer is that it immediately gets to the heart of the problem: you have wandered away from the shepherd. Christian pursuits and activities may well surround you, but you have lost sight of the shepherd, who is Jesus.

In the parable of the lost sheep in Luke 15, Jesus talked about the shepherd leaving the whole flock to go and find the one lost sheep. This clearly demonstrates that 'Come and get me' is a prayer that Jesus loves to answer, and there is not a single sheep he does not miss!

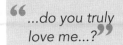

...do you truly love me...?

John 21.15

Healing and memories

When Jesus met with Peter after the resurrection, he asked him three times whether he loved him. It is almost possible to feel Peter's frustration as the same question kept coming. It is likely that Jesus asked Peter three times in order to mirror the three times Peter had denied him: Jesus was seeking to influence Peter's memory of what happened.

We all have painful memories. How can Jesus help by healing or touching them? Certainly the events of the past cannot be changed, but what can alter is the effect of them on us. Often it becomes possible to revisit the event in your mind, but instead of wondering where Jesus was, the episode can be seen through the perspective of his presence.

If there is a particular memory which is painful for you and you want to revisit it in the hope of finding healing, choose a quiet, safe place where you can ponder what happened. Ask yourself where Jesus is for you in this memory? You may have to 'look around' to find him, but the truth is that there has never been a moment when he was not present, so he is definitely there. Engage with his presence by asking yourself what difference it makes having him there? How does his presence affect you? What can you hold on to from this experience with Jesus in order to bring a lasting change?

Oi, you! | 1

In this invitation, a word that is missing from many translations is one of the most powerful. It is a word which can be translated as a loud shout, along the lines of "Oi, you!"

If someone yelled this loudly in your general direction, your attention would be caught and you would probably pay attention to what they wanted to say. This is exactly what God was seeking to do through Isaiah in this passage: he was getting the attention of every person who was thirsty. This was not a quiet word whispered in the ear of someone specific, but rather a loud call to all the people who might like to stand before the fountain of life and receive what was on offer.

All too often you may read some wonderful promises in the Bible and wonder if such words can really be for you. Does God really mean to include you in what he is offering? The answer is usually 'yes'. You would probably like every promise to have your own name at the beginning so you would know for certain it was meant for you. However, the Bible may have a different approach and if you can identify with the need, then the promise is there for you to explore.

> "...you who have no money, come, buy and eat!"

Isaiah 55.1

Learning to receive | 2

Jesus never said only good people would be recipients of his touch. In fact, in this verse from Isaiah those with nothing are being invited to receive. The Bible provides us with many instances of Jesus touching and blessing people who were far from good, Zacchaeus being a prime example. He was a tax collector who probably made a small fortune from abusing his position, right up until the moment when Jesus touched him. His change of heart came later.

Many of us tend to think we have to try to be good before God will touch us, when in reality his touch needs to come first. It is only this touch of God that is going to change our attitudes, so perhaps all we have to bring to the table of God's riches is our honesty. Knowing we need God is a major step towards receiving his touch.

We are so quick to assume we have to bargain for the things of God: "If you touch me, then I will do something in return." What he would rather hear from us are words such as, "I cannot help myself; I need you."

If you are hungry or desperate for something from God, it really isn't a problem if you are unable to do anything about it yourself. If you could do it, you wouldn't need God. Hold your hunger and thirst before God now. Be honest in your needs and be open to his touch.

Following your instincts

> *You and your brother Jews may then do whatever seems best with the rest of the silver and gold, in accordance with the will of your God.*
>
> **Ezra 7.18**

Do you ever tend to think God has drawn up a blueprint for your life which is locked away somewhere in heaven, and your task down here is to discover these plans and live your life accordingly? The potential for getting it wrong seems to be quite large! However, the will of God is not quite like this.

These words from Ezra provide some relief. The context is that some money had been given, along with instructions about how some of it was to be spent. There was an amount left over and it is about this that Ezra gave the instructions in today's verse, basically saying, do what seems best to you.

If you spend all your time seeking for God's specific will for every stage of the day ahead, you will actually miss out on so many opportunities to do good and bring something of the presence of God to those in need around you. It may be that there isn't a specific blueprint for each day which has to be followed to the letter, and perhaps part of your response to the wonder of God is for you to do what seems best to you.

Look at the hours ahead and decide how you can bring something of God to those you will meet. Just do it!

> '...he has compassion on all he has made.'
>
> **Psalm 145.9**

Keep your focus

As we lift people up in intercession, this verse can be a source of hope for us. Often we can feel as if we literally have to plead people's causes before God, that we have to persuade him how much they really need and deserve his touch. The truth is, of course, God knows full well how much they really need him, and he also has a love and compassion for them that outweighs anything we may feel.

Beginning times of prayer with a focus on God's incredible love for you is really helpful, as the effect is to release you from the strain of thinking you have to earn the favour of God. In a similar way, to begin times of intercession with the assurance of his unending and unyielding compassion for those for whom you pray can set a whole new tone for your intercession. Rather than beginning your prayers with pleading, they flow from a position of trust in his love.

This can change everything. Your immediate focus has been taken off the problem or person for whom you are praying, and has been firmly put back on God and his loving heart. This is a wonderful way to start prayer!

Bringing pleasure to the Holy Spirit

'And do not grieve the Holy Spirit of God ... Get rid of all bitterness, rage and anger, brawling and slander, along with every form of malice.'

Ephesians 4.30–31

It is interesting that Paul tells us not to grieve the Holy Spirit, and then goes on to list a range of actions all to do with our relationships with other people. In other words, grieving the Holy Spirit is not so much about our words and actions to him directly, but rather about how he takes offence at our attitude to other people.

Presumably the reverse is also true. If we are seeking to bring pleasure to the Holy Spirit, it is not so much about the praise and worship we offer to him, or whether we have the correct theological understanding of his relationship with the Father and the Son, but rather about how we are treating those around us. If bitterness and rage grieve the Holy Spirit, then forgiveness and love must bring him pleasure.

The good news is that this very day you will have many, many opportunities to bring pleasure to the Holy Spirit. If you fail, or simply forget, there will be plenty more chances! It is not arrogant or boastful to sit in his presence at the end of the day, or the next day, and ask him to bring to your mind those occasions when you gave him pleasure.

> *'But now you have rejected and humbled us'*
>
> **Psalm 44.9**

Sowing into tomorrow

The pain and anguish of the author are evident in this psalm. It begins by looking back over the past when things were going well, but in the middle there is a change to consider the author's present situation, where defeat and misery seem prevalent. What is worse for him is that in all his searching he is unable to see a reason for this suffering. It is not as if the people were being rebellious or wicked, and yet still there was suffering.

It may be you can relate to this psalm as you look back to a time when things were going considerably better than now. Perhaps you may be utterly unable to work out why things should be as bad as they are, or why your cries for help seem to elicit no response from God.

One of the most remarkable things in this psalm is the author's ability to cling to the wonder of God's love, despite the pain and confusion of his situation. His final words in the psalm are a declaration of God's unfailing love: 'Rise up and help us; redeem us because of your unfailing love.' Such a declaration is not made lightly and it comes out of a lifelong relationship with God.

This highlights the necessity of spending time every day reflecting on the wonder of God's love for you, not simply because it benefits you today, but also because of what it sows into tomorrow and the days ahead. Take some time to do this now.

God is always there

The land is still ours

2 Chronicles 14.7

Many years after the Israelites had entered the land God had given them, and after many periods of uprising and rebellion, the king decided to build up and fortify some of the towns. He recognised that despite the passing of time and the many challenges, nothing had really changed; the land still belonged to them and it was still God's gift to his people.

There may be times when you sense you are not as close to the Lord as you once were, possibly due to business, neglect, family commitments or even a period of rebellion. Yet this truth rings out: the land is still yours. All God's promises are still there for you; his forgiveness, love, gentleness and concern are waiting for you to return to them.

It is tempting to think you need to do something significant to find God again, such as a period of deep repentance, yet the first step is to stand firm on this beautiful truth. He has not removed any of his love and care from you; the land is still yours. Wherever you wander, he is still your God. If you feel you have wandered away, come back to this love that is as strong now as it has ever been.

> *...God, who gives life to everything*

1 Timothy 6.13

Letting God be at work

You probably have plans for the day ahead. In some areas it is quite easy to see how God could work, whereas in others it is more difficult to see what he might do. The natural tendency is to focus on moments you may be dreading, or which cause you anxiety, but this causes difficulties because you are looking at events from your perspective rather than from the possibility of what God could do.

This verse is so encouraging to take into the day ahead: 'God, who gives life to everything.' Why not let your plans run through your mind, and at each different event apply these words to it. In doing this, you are increasing your awareness of God's power to work in every situation, as these words proclaim not only that God will be there, but also that he gives life to everything. If there is life, there is hope, and you can enter the hours ahead with joy and peace rather than fear.

Kindness personified

" ...he is kind to the ungrateful and wicked.**"**
Luke 6.35

The kindness of God is not something we often think about. We talk about God's love, but this can be defined in all manner of ways, whereas to talk of the kindness of God is different.

The kindness of God is perfectly exemplified in Jesus, whose kindness was demonstrated in his ministry of going about doing good things – healing the sick, showing love and offering forgiveness – without first demanding a change in lifestyle.

The Bible tells us he hasn't changed; Jesus is the same today (Hebrews 13.8). The one who lives in us, and to whom we call out, is kind. He cannot change who he is; kindness is his nature.

As you sit in his presence for a few moments today, it's wonderful to think of him as loving, but also be aware you are sitting in the presence of kindness personified. It does not matter what you have been like, his desire is to be kind to you.

The power of worship

"O LORD, God of our fathers, are you not the God who is in heaven? You rule over all the kingdoms of the nations. Power and might are in your hand, and no one can withstand you."

2 Chronicles 20.6

When King Jehoshaphat offered these words of praise to God, it was not in the safe environment of a service; a vast army had come against him. His first instinct was to turn to God, and his prayer is beautiful. He does not dive straight into panicky prayers, but begins with worship.

Furthermore, he did not simply begin with worship because that seemed to be a good idea and what ought to be done at the beginning of prayer time. What his worship did was to set a marker that became a more fundamental truth than the immediate threat he faced.

You may not face armies coming against you, but you will probably face difficulties today, and you might be afraid or anxious. This is the time to worship.

Worship is choosing to proclaim the opposite of your fears, and to allow this truth to change you rather than let your fears overwhelm your life. This is what Jehoshaphat did. He saw an opposing army coming against him and he took his stand by proclaiming the power and might of the Lord. It would have been so easy to begin by proclaiming the power and might of the enemy, but that would probably have increased the scale of fear felt by everyone there. By proclaiming the opposite, the power and might of the Lord, faith was allowed to conquer fear and God responded by performing a miracle.

The mission carries on | 1

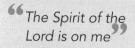

> **"** *The Spirit of the Lord is on me* **"**
>
> **Luke 4.18**

There is a landmark moment in the ministry of Jesus which is described by Luke in chapter 4 of his Gospel. At the beginning of his ministry Jesus went into a synagogue and found the reading he wanted to use as the basis for his talk. The passage he chose came from Isaiah 61 and Luke records the reading for us along with snippets of the talk Jesus gave. Perhaps the most powerful words are those Jesus used to begin his talk: "Today this scripture is fulfilled in your hearing."

In these words Jesus seemed to be saying that this reading is what would mark out his ministry and set the scene for what people could expect from him. The biggest challenge for us is that these words still apply. As you find the presence of Jesus, the one in whose presence you stand is the same Jesus who stood up in that synagogue in Luke 4. He still has the same mission, the same vision and the same heart.

As we spend time over the next few days pondering aspects of this vision which he revealed, try to find the excitement that this is the same Jesus who is with you constantly, and this message is still his heart for you.

> **"** *...he has anointed me to preach good news to the poor.* **"**
>
> **Luke 4.18**

Good news to the poor | 2

What is poverty? We may look at people who struggle to make a living in a third world slum area or whose lives are being destroyed by failing seasonal rains, and in comparison we may be embarrassed to use the word 'poor'. However, if poverty is about being unable to meet our own needs, then there are areas in which we may admit to being poor. It may be that you are in material need, or perhaps you feel you have no control over sickness, oppression, memories of the past, or a host of other things. As you think about poverty in this way, the phrase 'good news to the poor' becomes a foretaste of the other things Jesus went on to speak about in the passage from Isaiah 61.

The anointing on Jesus was to bring good news to the poor, to tell them that although they were lacking in some way, their need was not the bottom line. Whatever your need, Jesus is the good news. He is your Messiah, provider, healer, strengthener and deliverer.

Take a moment to ask yourself where Jesus is for you right now, and as you find his presence be honest with him about your need at this time. Where is your poverty? What is it you are unable to do for yourself? Speak to him and listen out for his reply – that picture, Bible verse or spontaneous thought which comes into your mind – and in this way find the Messiah who has come to bring good news to the poor – to you.

A new life! | 3

Without going into the intricacies of miscarriages of justice, prisoners are usually prisoners because they have done something wrong. In some way they are to blame for the situation in which they find themselves. The temptation is for us to think, 'You've made your bed, now lie in it!'

The attitude of Jesus could not be more different. Freedom for the prisoners is a startling revelation of his mission. We might think this is unjust: why should people find freedom from the consequences of their actions when they deserve what they are going through? How can Jesus be so good to those who do not deserve it? We will probably begin to change our attitude when we find that Jesus applied this principle across the board – even to us.

This is what forgiveness is about. It means we are not treated as our sins deserve, and neither is anyone else. The foulest of sinners is offered forgiveness, and so are we. What he does for others is what he offers to us. It's not so much, 'You've made your bed now lie in it,' but rather, 'Take up your bed and walk!'

Is there something from your past making you feel like a prisoner? Jesus' vision for you is freedom, and the way you can discover this is by beginning to believe and accept that it is for you. You really are forgiven.

Healing | 4

> "He has sent me to proclaim... recovery of sight for the blind"
>
> **Luke 4.18**

It is easy to suggest this verse refers simply to a renewal of an inner vision, but even a cursory reading of the Gospels reveals a picture of Jesus who spent much time healing the physically ill – individuals, groups and sometimes whole crowds. It is no surprise to discover that this is something he said at the start of his ministry that he would do.

It is a mistake to limit Jesus' promise of physical healing to what we might think of as the more formal healing ministry of the church. Jesus uses human skills and agencies to bring about his purposes, as well as supernatural means. His statement gives us real hope. The Bible never says Jesus told the sick to rejoice in their illnesses. He didn't seem to make a connection between the suffering that was inevitable and the sickness he saw in the people to whom he ministered. His words and actions gave hope.

If you are in mental, physical or spiritual pain, you can call out to Jesus with confidence, knowing he is not rejoicing in your pain or delighting in your suffering. Call out in the certainty that it is good and proper to call out to him for healing.

Bringing what is above to what is below | 5

He has sent me... to release the oppressed

Luke 4.18

If prisoners suffer because of what they have done themselves, then perhaps we can think of the oppressed as those whose suffering is not due to their own actions, but rather because of the actions of others.

If you are oppressed by abuse – physical, verbal or mental – the effect may be to cause barriers to go up, and you find yourself cut off from the world around you. Alternatively, the oppression may take the form of years of being gradually ground down so you no longer sense the value you are to God and to others.

The ministry of Jesus is to bring release. In Ephesians 1.22 Paul wrote that everything was beneath Jesus' feet and this is the basis from which he brings about this release. He is seated above absolutely everything, and yet comes to our level to bring what is above to what is below.

As you seek release, a good place to start is to let your act of worship be to acknowledge Jesus is above every form of oppression you have suffered. Whatever it might be, it has not bound him or shackled him in any way and he is still the Lord. Yet he does not stay in heaven looking down upon your suffering; he stands with you in love and power to bring you release.

> **He has sent me...** to proclaim the year of the Lord's favour.**

Luke 4.19

The special time is now! | 6

If you are going through hardships of any sort, a reasonable question is whether God actually wants to help you at this time? We have all heard stories of God helping some people in wonderful ways, but when times are hard it feels as though those he doesn't help outweigh those he does. This can lead us to conclude that there are special people whom God touches, or special times and places where he seems to do more.

The concluding line to the reading Jesus chose to read in the synagogue proclaims a different way of thinking. There are special times, and now is one of them; there are special people and one of them is you; and there are special places and you are in one right now.

Often a first step to finding God's touch is to recapture a sense of hope – hope that you are included in his promises and are not forgotten by him. As you begin to pray, find a sense of Jesus enthroned above all things and proclaim to yourself that this vision is for you now.

This is for us | 7

" *Today this scripture is fulfilled in your hearing.* **"**

Luke 4.21

When Jesus finished reading this passage from Isaiah 61, he began to talk about it. The words he chose to begin his sermon were electrifying: "Today this scripture is fulfilled in your hearing." Jesus was saying that this is what could be expected of him, this is what he came to do. He was speaking both to those listening in the temple in a bygone age and to us today.

Does this mean he will do whatever you ask of him right now? Not necessarily, but what it does mean is that whoever you are and wherever you might be, Jesus stands with you right now, still with this same mission he had when he proclaimed these words in the synagogue two thousand years ago.

Jesus' proclamation did not mean that every person who was sick was healed in his three years of ministry (the disciples were still healing the sick in Jerusalem even after the time of Jesus) but it does mean that from then on Jesus' ministry was released and it continues to this very day. His words still stand and his promises still count, because Jesus is still among us, encouraging us to believe it can be different.

Things can be different for you. Bring yourself and your needs to the one who spoke these words for you, and stand before him in expectation.

> 'I have no greater joy than to hear that my children are walking in the truth.'
>
> **3 John 4**

Walking in the truth

We all walk in something! What will you be walking in today? It may be you are in despair, or perhaps full of joy, hopeful about something or clinging on to your faith. One of the biggest decisions we all have to make is whether we walk in the truth or in a lie.

To walk in the truth is to live your life believing you are uniquely loved by God, that Jesus came to do everything he could to reveal the Father's heart to you and that you will never be alone for a moment, since the Holy Spirit lives within you. You probably know these things to be generally true, but to walk in them is to believe they are specifically true for you personally.

If you do not walk in this truth, it is not the case that you walk in a mellow 'no-man's-land'. The danger is that you soon find yourself walking in a lie, believing that God does not love you and is not with you. You do not need to consciously walk in a lie – it happens automatically when you do not walk in the truth.

Lay aside the difficulties and situations you may be facing and instead dwell on the glorious truths that God has revealed through the Bible: you are wonderfully and uniquely loved by God; he loved you so much he gave Jesus for you; and in you dwells the wonder of the presence of the Holy Spirit. Hold on to these truths and walk in them today.

God's love for us

'*How great is the love the Father has lavished on us, that we should be called children of God!*'

1 John 3.1

There is an old saying, 'Familiarity breeds contempt.' This can often be true of our Christian lives and the great truths revealed in the Bible.

Sometimes you may speak to God and call him 'Father', using the term easily and without too much thought. In doing so, you can quickly forget how this one word is a stunning revelation of just how much you are loved and cherished. Every time you refer to God as 'Father', this sums up all the love he has for you; as you call him 'Father', he calls you 'Child'.

To be called God's child is so releasing and liberating. At times, you may think of him calling you a 'disappointment' or 'failure', because these are the words spoken by others, but it is simply not true. God calls you 'child' because he loves you and because he desperately wants you to know how loved you are. Whatever the world may call you, he speaks the word 'child' to you with great tenderness.

As you speak the word 'Father' to him, be aware of him calling you 'Child'.

Shining where we are

> *"Whoever can be trusted with very little can also be trusted with much"*
>
> **Luke 16.10**

What is it that has been entrusted to you? It is all too easy to look around at people you admire and feel quite overwhelmed at what some of them manage to get done and the way they do it. You might then turn your eyes on yourself and wonder if you are doing anything worthwhile in comparison.

We all have our own lives and responsibilities, and the question is not how well we match up to other people, but how well we match up to what we have been given. You might think what you have been entrusted with is small compared to the responsibilities of others, but this is what has been given to you. The question is how well will you do with what God has given you?

So what has God given you and what are the things over which you have influence? You might think of family, work, the way you use your time or a ministry you undertake. In your opinion, these things may not be terribly significant, but they are God's gift to you, and in every situation in which God has set you, there is the opportunity to let something of God shine.

Take a moment to mull over the things that God has entrusted to you. What will you do with them today?

No condemnation

These words are so well known, and because of this it is easy to miss the impact of them. One way to recapture their freshness is to take out the word 'world' and replace it with your name or the name of someone else: 'God loved me so much that he gave Jesus. God did not send Jesus to condemn me, but to save me.' Take a moment to do this and let the truth of these words sink in.

> *For God so loved the world that he gave his one and only Son, that whoever believes in him shall not perish but have eternal life. For God did not send his Son into the world to condemn the world, but to save the world through him.*
>
> **John 3.16–17**

So often we speak of God's love, but we actually live under condemnation although it was never God's intention to make us feel this way. It may be that our sins or weaknesses are revealed, but the next stage is always the offer of change, a life of freedom rather than a journey of guilt that leaves us feeling as though we are behind prison bars.

Freedom begins by seeing the hand of Jesus outstretched to you personally with an offer to lift you out of the pit, and this begins when you take his words of love personally and seriously.

Let these words sink in deeper: 'Because God loved me, he sent Jesus for me. Jesus came to save me and not to condemn me.'

Imitators of God

This phrase seems to be a lofty command to which we feel we will never aspire – one of those commands we can never possibly hope to obey. Yet within it is some wonderful good news.

The key to understanding this phrase is the single word that comes next, the word 'therefore', which refers back to the preceding verses at the end of Ephesians 4. In this passage, Paul had encouraged his readers in a number of things: to speak well of each other, get rid of all bitterness and be kind and compassionate to one another. It is at this point he goes on to say, 'Be imitators of God, therefore…' In other words, he was asking them to be the same as God.

This is the wonderful news, a real revelation of God's character. It means God is just like this towards you:

God speaks well of you.

God thinks well of you. He is not constantly wringing his hands in desperation about you.

God is not bitter towards you. He does not store up a record of your wrongdoing, thinking of new ways to trip you up.

God is kind and compassionate to you. He is looking for ways to bless you and probably carries out acts of kindness for you throughout the day without you really noticing.

Being an imitator of God is not an impossible challenge. It is an invitation to gaze in wonder at the God who loves you.

Opposition

> *But we prayed to our God and posted a guard day and night to meet this threat.*
>
> **Nehemiah 4.9**

Nehemiah had been entrusted with a great work rebuilding the walls of Jerusalem. God called him for this task and was behind him, yet there was still opposition.

We are all involved in doing the work of God in different ways. You may be involved in a particular ministry to which you sense you have been called, or are seeking to serve him as a husband, wife or parent. Perhaps you are rebuilding your life, seeking to walk away from the past with all its destruction and walk into the future to which God calls you.

It would be encouraging if everything went swimmingly well, and there is a logic that if God wants a job done, then surely he will make it easy. Throughout the Bible, however, it seems as if the work of God and opposition go hand in hand. Opposition may take many forms, ranging from people who are against you to feelings such as fear, uncertainty and doubt.

However, what is important to note is that opposition, in whatever form, does not mean you have got it wrong. Far from it! As you battle those things standing against you, it is good to remember you are standing in an incredibly long line of people who have also faced opposition, but have found the joy of being a co-worker with God. In spite of any opposition that you might be feeling, reassure yourself of your calling with these words: 'I am God's co-worker.'

> *Let us go to the house of the LORD.*

Psalm 122.1

Building a house for God to live in

At times you are certain to face uncertainty and confusion. Your physical surroundings may be the same but circumstances may change; concerns may crowd in and perceived threats arise. What do you do? 'Go to the house of the Lord.'

This is not so much about physically going to a church or a different place, but about taking a moment to find the spiritual core within you. It is much easier to do this if time has already been invested storing up God's resources in your heart, as these have laid the foundations for his house to be built within you.

Repeating a Bible verse is one way of doing this, so that when something unexpected arises during the day these verses come readily to mind. Then it is more natural to 'go to the house of the Lord' where you can draw upon his presence and wait for him to show you a way through your difficulty.

There are many other helpful phrases, such as:
'I bear your name, LORD God Almighty.'
'My body is a temple of the Holy Spirit.'
'I believe you are the Christ, the Son of God who comes into the world.'
'Lord Jesus Christ, have mercy on me.'

Sometimes you may need to 'go to the house of the Lord' several times in a day, so make sure you have built a house to go to.

Giving and receiving

> **"**...you also should wash one another's feet.**"**
>
> **John 13.14**

Implicit in Jesus' command for us to wash one another's feet is the willingness to let our own feet be washed. It can be easier to minister to others, both spiritually or practically, and hard to receive ministry ourselves or help from other people. Perhaps the reason for this is because we simply do not like to reveal our weaknesses, as we are not sure what people will think of us. Or maybe we are not sure whether we are allowed to be weak, as the more spiritual we are, surely the stronger and more self-sufficient we should be.

The truth is that it is fine to be weak. In fact, Paul wrote about rejoicing in his weaknesses because he knew they were a doorway for God's strength to shine through him. If Paul had denied his weaknesses (like many of us do), then he would have missed out on so much of the wonder of God.

One way we can begin to experience the strength of God in our weaknesses is to ask God for help so that his strength can flow through others to us.

> *In faithfulness he will bring forth justice; he will not falter or be discouraged till he establishes justice on earth.*
>
> **Isaiah 42.3–4**

His vision of justice

Unanswered prayer is something we have all experienced. There will probably have been times when you have poured out your heart before him, only to be disappointed and confused when your prayers seem to be to no avail. However, none of us have any idea what God really does in response to our prayers.

Yet this verse shows us something of God's on-going mission to bring justice to all in need, and the assurance that nothing will get in the way of this. In one sense, it is possible to bring this quest for justice into everything Jesus does: his healing ministry is about bringing to people the abundant life God wants for them; his teaching on wealth and riches is about releasing people from the prison of their own possessions; and his giving of himself to release forgiveness is about setting people free from the chains of bitterness and resentment.

From our perspective, there may indeed be times when we simply do not understand the ways in which God acts – and some of these ways appear to be almost unjust – but part of our journey of faith is to hold on to this revealed vision of Jesus. Bringing about justice is Jesus' goal and nothing will get in the way.

As you look ahead at all you plan to do, be aware that Jesus has another agenda: to work within you and through you, bringing forth his kingdom and justice.

Unlimited possibilities

> *Jesus replied, "What is impossible with men is possible with God."*
>
> **Luke 18.27**

Logically, this verse must be true, because the Almighty God of heaven and earth must have far greater power than us humans. However, when Jesus made this statement he was not simply speaking about the vast gulf separating God and man. He was talking about the action of God towards all men and women.

Jesus had been speaking about rich people's attitudes towards God and the truth that it was so hard for those who had everything to turn to God. It was in this context that Jesus stated that nothing was impossible with God; he could even break into the mindsets and attitudes of the wealthy and bring about dramatic changes of heart.

This is what you can take into your day: there is no situation into which God cannot break and no person who is beyond his reach. Out of his profound care for you he is willing to be your God, not at your beck and call, but to reveal his glory through you and to prompt a deeper surrender within you.

Take a few minutes to bring the difficult things in your life to God and say over each of them, "For me this may be impossible, but nothing is impossible with God."

> *'...he looked towards heaven...'*
>
> **John 17.1**

What are you looking at?

When John wrote these words about Jesus, did he record what he actually saw (perhaps Jesus physically looking upwards) or was he trying to convey Jesus' attitude, some sort of change in Jesus' focus? Whichever it was, the lesson is the same: when you pray, look to God and not to the things you are holding in prayer.

It is all too easy to start to pray but actually your attention is on the issues confronting you, such as anxiety or sickness. This may not seem so bad, but it misses out on something very important – that of fixing your attention first on the Father who loves you.

Once you become accustomed to beginning your prayers by reminding yourself of the Father's love, then your initial focus is more likely to be the enormity of God, rather than the enormity of your problems. What you focus on is going to be magnified, so if this is the wonder and power of God, the way you pray will be dramatically affected.

Who is praying for you?

‘Therefore he is able to save completely those who come to God through him, because he always lives to intercede for them.’

Hebrews 7.25

This is written about us! We have come to God through Jesus, who lives to intercede for us. This incredible concept of Jesus praying for us takes on an even more amazing dimension with the realisation of the nature of who is doing the praying; this is not some weak, ineffectual prayer, but the intercessions of the Lord of heaven and earth. The one praying for you is the one through whom the world was created and is sustained. He is the one who loved you to such an extent that he gave his life for you. He is the one who, with a word, called forth Lazarus from the grave, and with another word stilled the storm.

In moments of desperation you may wonder who could possibly help you, but at that very moment of wondering, there is, in fact, someone already praying for you who has experienced all you have experienced, who loves you more than you can comprehend and who has access to power greater than you can imagine.

In times of need, it may be that you have no idea what to pray. In this case, all you need to do is to turn your heart to Jesus simply by saying his name. In calling out his name, not only does he hear your cry, he is already engaged in prayer for you.

Still yourself by speaking his name, and catch the vision of him praying for you right now.

Fighting to hold on to God's treasures

In this sad saga from the history of the kings of Israel and Judah gold shields were plundered from the Temple, and the king replaced them with bronze shields. He then made a great show of guarding them but, compared to what he once had, they were worthless.

It is sad to replace the wonder of what God has given us with something else. He has given us the reality of his presence, the assurance of forgiveness, the promise of unfailing love and the revelation of just how precious we are to him. Yet all too often we find that such things have been plundered from us, and rather than fight to get them back we settle for less.

At times we may look back and realise we have let slip the wonder of God's love for us. We may sing about it in church, but we have stopped taking seriously the reality of his love for us. We pay lip service to the truth of God being with us without taking the time to seek his presence in any given situation in our lives. We find ourselves thinking about our identity in negative ways, perhaps concentrating more on what we do not have rather than on what we do have. These truths are worth returning to every day. If you sense they have been plundered from you, fight to recapture them.

Never-ending grace

'The grace was given us in Christ Jesus before the beginning of time'

2 Timothy 1.9

God loved us enough to send Jesus, but does he ever get fed up with us? Does God ever look at you and change his mind about loving you? This verse from Paul's letter to Timothy is a reminder of the on-going, unchanging nature of the grace of God. Since time began, the unalterable plan of God for his people was to pour out grace and reveal his unconditional love. With the coming of Jesus, God was able to do this fully and provide the certainty that he would never change his mind. No matter what the situation, the answer is always going to be the undeserved love of God.

Are there times when you have forgotten God? If so, his reply is to pour out his grace. Are there times when you have sinned? His reply is to pour out his grace. Is there something for which you long to cry out in prayer? Again, his answer is to pour out his grace.

God longs for you to take his grace seriously, to honour and call upon it. It was never his plan for you to try to get by without it.

Being suitably clothed

'You are all sons of God through faith in Christ Jesus, for all of you who were baptised into Christ have clothed yourselves with Christ.'

Galatians 3.26–27

These words were not an opportunity by Paul to get into a debate about the mechanics of what constitutes a real baptism (this was one of the legalistic arguments Paul was encouraging his listeners to avoid). Instead, what Paul is trying to get across is the truth of what happens to those people who put their trust in Jesus. He speaks of them being 'clothed' with Jesus.

What a beautiful picture this word evokes: as you step into the day or hours ahead, you wear Jesus whether you feel it or not. Everything upon him is upon you; you simply need to turn your awareness to what is already there. If you need courage, remember that you are clothed with Jesus and all his courage. Perhaps it is wisdom you need, in which case you are clothed with the wisdom of Jesus. Are you in need of strength? If so, you are clothed with Jesus and all his strength. If you find yourself in moments of real need, come back to this truth that you carry the very presence of God.

Consciously draw from the presence of Jesus what you need for each moment of each day.

Being in God's will

'...pursue righteousness, godliness, faith, love, endurance and gentleness.'

1 Timothy 6.11

We often ask God what he wants us to do in a particular situation, but this verse clearly lays out God's desire for us and the qualities he wants us to exhibit. If you are ever at a loss to know what you should be doing at any given time, run through this list and seek to pursue these qualities, as they will bring you right back to the heart of God's will for you.

Are you receiving God's righteousness based not on your goodness but on what Jesus did on the cross for you? Is your speech and behaviour godly? Do you remind yourself regularly that he loves you and has chosen you? When you are in contact with others, are you seeking to manifest his love and care for them? Are you holding on to what you believe, even if it seems a hard thing to do in your current circumstances? At this very moment, are you exhibiting gentleness, both to others and to yourself?

If you are seeking to put these things into practice, you will never be far away from what God wants for you. He is quite able to communicate his specific will in any situation, but in the meantime God's will is always that you live in his love and let it flow through you.

God longs to touch you

John 4.6–7

'...Jesus, tired as he was from the journey, sat down by the well. It was about the sixth hour. When a Samaritan woman came to draw water, Jesus said to her, "Will you give me a drink?"'

In Jesus' time, Jews and Samaritans disagreed over many religious matters, so it was quite natural for Jewish people to regard the Samaritans as somewhat different. The Bible gives us several stories – such as the story of the Good Samaritan and the tale of the one leper who returned to Jesus to give thanks – where it is considered slightly surprising that a Samaritan would behave in such a way. This verse refers to another profound encounter between Jesus and a Samaritan woman, who would not normally be expected to feature at the centre of a story.

You may also sometimes feel you are not the sort of person Jesus would touch. You may not think of yourself as particularly devout, and life is probably a bit of a struggle. Sometimes it can be tempting to wonder if God really notices you.

The truth is that you are exactly the sort of person Jesus notices, and this story of the woman at the well illustrates how Jesus deliberately went out of his way to engage with someone who probably felt sidelined. Perhaps one of the reasons for this account is so that you can be encouraged to approach Jesus with the joy of knowing he actually came for you. You matter; he has seen you and he knows you are here.

Praising when you don't feel like it! | 1

'...all my inmost being, praise his holy name.'

Psalm 103.1

Psalm 103 is a beautiful psalm that seems to share God's heart with us. Over the coming days we are going to look at a number of phrases in this psalm and discover some of the riches it holds for us.

When you are happy and thankful, or enjoying singing songs of praise in church, you probably find it very natural to praise God. The challenge in this phrase is the simple word 'all': every part of you can turn to him in worship, including the bits of you that aren't feeling joyful. Genuine praise is praising God when you don't feel like it, as well as when you do.

God does not demand your praise because he needs it, but because he knows that if your heart is turned to him in worship, things inside you will change. It is the times when you do not feel like worshipping that have the potential to become transforming times for you. When things have gone wrong, or if you have sinned or when something bad has happened – these are the times to begin to worship God. You may still hurt or have questions, but whatever has happened to you, God has not changed and as you begin to worship him, something in your heart moves closer to him.

The situations around you may or may not change, but worship opens a door to God's presence.

God's benefits | 2

This psalm began with a call for every part of us to praise him and now it continues, 'forget not all his benefits'.

The root of the word 'benefits' can also be translated as 'dealings'. It is about what flows from God. Over the next few days we shall be looking in more detail at what does flow from him. The point is that God is not some remote figure who created this world long ago, and nor is Jesus a wonderful figure from history whose memory is enshrined in stained glass windows. The wonder of God is that he is a living God, alive and present for us today, who longs to be approached so that he can pour out his active love upon us.

The 'benefits' and 'dealings' we will look at are not like presents that drop from the sky, but instead flow from the living God. The words Jesus spoke in Matthew 11.28, "Come to me", ring out to all of us. He is alive and wants you to come to him because he has so much to give you.

When you pray you probably like to use your own style and practice of prayer, but before you begin, call to mind that you are actually approaching the living God and coming into his very presence.

Forgiving yourself | 3

'...who forgives all your sins...'

Psalm 103.3

God does not sweep your sins under a carpet or brush them off as if they never happened. He forgives them, and he has paid the price for them so they can never be put back upon you. God is not selective about which sins he forgives; Jesus paid for them all. It is more a question of which sins you are willing to let go of.

Forgiving yourself is one of the hardest things to do, and it is so easy to continue to carry the burden of sin even though Jesus has totally paid for it.

If you still feel burdened about things in your past, try this exercise. Draw an outline of a cross on a sheet of paper. Within the outline write down the particular sins you feel burdened by. In writing down these words, you are transferring your sin from yourself to the cross. Now destroy the piece of paper: rip it up, throw it away, burn it – anything to demonstrate that those sins have been removed from you. Jesus has taken them away.

who ... heals all your diseases

Psalm 103.3

God's agenda | 4

So much of the Gospels is taken up with Jesus' ministry of healing, and yet when we pray for healing we do not see as much as we would like. Why not? We are told in John 14.12, "...anyone who has faith in me will do what I have been doing", which suggests that Jesus saw his ministry of healing continuing into the future. So why don't we see more healing?

One reason is that our very impatience for healing may distract us from what else God is seeking to do in our lives. Certainly there are occasions when Jesus did more than heal people. The woman who touched his cloak was healed, but he also wanted her to hear him call her 'daughter'. In John 9.35, Jesus deliberately went after a man who had been healed so he could reveal who he really was to him. Perhaps for you, too, there are other things God wants to do in your life? When you are in need, spend some time in his presence and ask him.

Jesus is committed to healing all your dis-eases, but it may be that he would like to do this in a different order to what you had in mind.

A helping hand to lift you up | 5

'...who redeems your life from the pit...'

Psalm 103.4

The amazing thing about being lifted out of a pit is that you aren't usually judged for being there in the first place. It may be that you slipped into a pit by accident, or perhaps you were pushed into the pit by others. Or it may be that whatever mess you are in is through your own deliberate fault and the only person you can blame is yourself.

The idea of being lifted up out of a pit is a theme to which Jesus would return. In Matthew 12.11, he referred to healing being as natural as lifting an animal out of a pit. This is the vision the psalmist gives us: there is life beyond the pit. It doesn't matter how you got there, the desire of Jesus is to lift you out of it.

The way out begins by understanding that God does not want you in the pit. He does not enjoy your suffering any more than you do and he wants you out of it. In what ways would you say you are in a pit? Focus on the sense that God derives no pleasure from you being there and pray from that perspective.

> *...who...crowns you with love and compassion*

Psalm 103.4

You're loved already! | 6

This line is a reminder that God's love and compassion are bestowed upon you by him, and are not things you have to work for or earn. The love of God is free, but perhaps most important of all it has already been poured out upon you. God is not still deciding whether or not to give it to you.

The Bible says that God chose to pour out his love upon you before the foundation of the world (Ephesians 1.4). In other words, before you had the chance to do anything right or wrong to make him change his mind you were loved, and nothing can change this. You may be tempted to look at your actions and assume they separate you from God's love, but Romans 8.38–39 makes it quite clear that there is nothing that can separate you from his love.

Take a moment to reflect on the amazing fact that whoever you are and whatever you feel you may have done, the living God loves you.

Are you satisfied? | 7

'...who satisfies your desires with good things...'

Psalm 103.5

This sounds a bit like a 'whoopee' verse – anything you want, you can have! However it is not quite saying this. The promise is satisfaction, and it is the things you want that will be satisfied. Yet such is the extent of God's love and power that he is able to bring deep satisfaction to the roots of your real desires, rather than simply to satisfy what you perceive your desires to be.

This might make God out to be a bit of a spoilsport, but if you think about it you may have had other dreams and desires that would have been disastrous if you had received what you thought you wanted. With his foresight, God is able to see beyond our desires to their root cause, and out of his care and love he brings satisfaction to these roots. It is often said that the deepest desire we all have is to know we are profoundly and deeply loved. Perhaps this is the greatest satisfaction God gives us.

As you bring your requests to God, it is worth asking what it is you really want. What lies at the heart of your requests to him?

> *'...your youth is renewed like the eagle's.'*
>
> **Psalm 103.5**

Renewing your vision | 8

The church would be so popular if it could promise to restore youth! Is God really promising an anti-ageing cure? Sadly not! Perhaps what this verse is alluding to is the recapturing of the visions we held when we were younger. To meet despondent and downcast youth can be quite depressing, but to meet youth with vision and passion can stir something within us. It is a tragedy when vision and passion are lost. One of the lovely by-products of having a renewed encounter with God is that our visions, dreams and passions can be renewed.

It is worth reflecting on what your dreams and visions were when you were younger, and what has happened to them? Have they been fulfilled or have they withered?

Bring these visions to Jesus and ask him to breathe his life upon these dreams that originated with him. No one is ever too old to be used and the Bible shows us remarkable examples of people serving God with passion despite advancing years. Abraham and Moses had their youth renewed by on-going encounters with the living God. Why not you?

Your cause is God's cause | 9

'The LORD works ... justice for all the oppressed.'
Psalm 103.6

Bringing about justice is a theme that Jesus picked up when he talked about prayer. In Luke 18 he told a story of a persistent widow and her attempts to gain justice from an unjust judge. The point of the parable was to encourage persistence in prayer and Jesus concluded with these words: "And will not God bring about justice for his chosen ones, who cry out to him day and night?" (Luke 18.6). No matter how long the process takes, and regardless of how bleak it may seem at times, God is as committed to bringing about justice as any just judge.

What are the things for which you are crying out in prayer? When you pray for things in line with God's word, you are crying out for justice. You may need to persevere, and no doubt along the way the content of your prayers may change as you discern more of God's heart, but your cause is God's cause because you are on his side. You are not working on your own, and God is working for you to bring about his purposes. Be encouraged and persevere; God is on your side.

God's claim about himself | 10

'The LORD is compassionate and gracious, slow to anger, abounding in love.'

Psalm 103.8

In this psalm, which we are told was written by David, we see him looking back on his life with God and recording some of the things he learned. These words, however, are not originally from David but from God himself. In Exodus 34.6 God promised to reveal himself to Moses, and as he passed by he spoke these same words that David repeats in this psalm. In other words, these words are not simply one man's opinion of what God is like, they are God's claim about himself and they reflect how he wants us to think of him.

Before you pray for anything in particular, it is worth spending a few moments before God slowly and thoughtfully repeating these words over and over until the truth of who God is sinks deeper in to you. Once you have done this you will find you can bring your requests to him with a new confidence in his love.

'You are compassionate and gracious, slow to anger, abounding in love.'

Come to God | 11

> ‘...he does not treat us as our sins deserve or repay us according to our iniquities.’
>
> **Psalm 103.10**

Life can seem very unfair at times and we are quick to spot injustices against us, especially when we feel we do not deserve them. However, this verse brings a whole new perspective: we probably do deserve many things, but God treats us with incredible kindness in spite of what we might have done wrong.

You have probably experienced times when you felt you have 'blown it' and perhaps felt unable to approach God before much soul-searching and repentance. It is exactly in these times that you should call this verse to mind and stand before him in wonder, At the same time, God is longing for you to come to him so that he can shine his wonderful light upon you and pour out his cleansing grace.

Why do we tend to hide away and stay in the darkness until we feel it is appropriate to come to God? Are we waiting for him to cool off or calm down? It is always the right time to come to him no matter who you are or what you have done.

Hear the words of Jesus spoken to you: "Come to me."

> '...as far as the east is from the west, so far has he removed our transgressions from us.'

Psalm 103.12

True forgiveness | 12

Sometimes it's tempting to think of forgiveness operating like a filing cabinet: when we confess our sins, they are removed from God's immediate gaze and filed away. The next time we sin the file is reopened and cross references are made with much tut-tutting on God's part. One day, we suspect, the file will be opened and all our sins will be laid before us for a final reckoning.

However, the reality of forgiveness is more like another piece of office hardware – a shredder! When sins are forgiven, it is as if they are shredded, never again to be used in evidence against us. The writer to the Hebrews reminds us of Jeremiah's words that God "will remember their sins no more." (Hebrews 8.12)

Forgiveness is for real. When Jesus took your sins upon himself, it was not a temporary reprieve or a filing exercise; it was a total once-for-all payment. The imagery of this phrase in the psalm is perfect; how much further could your wrong-doing be removed from you than as far as the east is from the west?

If you have confessed your sins, but still feel guilty, think about the filing cabinet and the shredder!

The Father of compassion | 13

> 'As a father has compassion on his children, so the LORD has compassion on those who fear him'
>
> **Psalm 103.13**

The concept of God as a loving father is not a made-up dream but a truth revealed in both the Old and New Testaments. In this psalm, David does not simply talk about God as a father but picks up on a particular aspect of fatherhood – compassion. We can be very quick to relate to God according to our own experience of fatherhood, especially if it is not a happy one. The sense behind the word 'compassion' is of a deep love or mercy. It is the very best possible experience of fatherhood, and it is there for us.

Jesus longs for you to enjoy the Father's love in just the same way he did. In John 17.26 he says that he has revealed the Father so that you can also share in this same loving relationship. When Jesus invites you to call God 'Father', he is inviting you to come to one who longs for you to discover that compassion for yourself.

Take some time to see yourself as a child being cradled by a loving parent. Let God be your parent.

Comfort in times of suffering

> *My comfort in my suffering is this: Your promise preserves my life.*
> **Psalm 119.50**

Comfort in suffering is more than just nice words, it is something that reaches deep inside and somehow touches our need and the pain. This psalmist found his attitude to the promises of God touched his suffering.

Sometimes, however, the promises of God can actually make us feel worse; it's like dangling something in front of us that we cannot achieve, and we begin to feel guilty.

The first step to finding joy, rather than frustration, in God's promises is to see his heart and desire reflected in them. The things he promises are first and foremost what he wants for us, his much loved children. He is not trying to lay out an obstacle course for us to claim these promises, but instead wants us to see that they reflect his very heart for us. Call to mind a promise from the Bible. As you study it, try to work out what this promise says about God's heart. The next step is to begin to worship God for who he is and what this promise says about him. By doing this, the promise itself is more likely to touch your heart and bring real comfort in your suffering.

Coming back to God

> " *...You have forsaken your first love.* "

Revelation 2.4

We would all like to think we are utterly faithful in our love for God at all times, but sadly this is probably not true, as our devotion to God goes through times of greater and lesser intensity. When we feel we have wandered, we may wonder what we can do to recapture our devotion and set out with all manner of resolutions to try to prove our sincerity.

Perhaps the most powerful thing you can do to restore or deepen your relationship with God is to grasp the fact that you may indeed forget your first love and waiver many times in your love for him, but he never waivers in his love for you. Grasping this simple fact can change everything. You are utterly loved by God and nothing you have done can ever change this. Jesus gave himself for you to prove his eternal love, and this cannot be taken back – it is done for all time.

To return to your first love for God is to return to his love for you, to dwell on it and to understand that it will always be about what he has done for you. Take a moment to do this now.

Being holy

'... be holy in all you do'

1 Peter 1.15

It is so easy to feel condemned by this verse because we rarely feel holy – and if we don't feel holy, how can we be holy in everything we do? When we come to reflect on the day, we all too often look back on our failings, which underline our feelings of unholiness!

A more helpful way of looking at the topic of holiness is to see it as the awareness of God's presence with you throughout the day. One definition of holiness is 'his life in us'. A wonderful verse to fall back on in every situation is this verse from Jeremiah 15.16: 'I bear your name, O LORD God Almighty.' If you can go through the next 24 hours with this verse as near to you as the breath you breathe, it has the potential to bring real change to you.

The truth contained in this verse is all about God's constant presence within you. It can strengthen you in times of temptation when you need to know his presence is there for you to draw upon, and it can bring you back to God to ask for his forgiveness, knowing that he is longing for you to return to his loving presence. His constant presence also opens up endless possibilities for you in the encounters you have with other people. You will have something to offer them that is beyond your own strength and wisdom.

Use Jeremiah's verse to find God's life and presence within you: 'I bear your name, O LORD God Almighty.'

Possessing the best

'The law from your mouth is more precious to me than thousands of pieces of silver and gold.'

Psalm 119.72

As far as this psalmist was concerned, what came from the mouth of God was worth more than a hoard of silver or gold. If you could choose between solid gold and the voice of God, you probably know which you ought to choose, but I wonder…!

Instead of listing why the voice of God might be better than gold, think about the possibility of this claim actually being true. What if you really do possess something of more value than gold?

It would certainly give you extra confidence if you went about your day with a thousand pieces of silver and gold in your possession, and yet the verse says you have more than this. You have God speaking to you, the promise of his presence with you and the assurance of his love. Somehow it seems harder to have as much confidence in these things as in a pocketful of gold. Yet these glorious truths are clearly stated and are as real as if you had bulging pockets.

Hold a coin in your hand right now and remind yourself that you have something more precious than a thousand coins. Whenever you reach into your pocket or bag for some money during the day ahead, try to remember you have something of priceless value in your possession, which could make more difference to you than anything else. You have the presence of God.

Stopping to ask

Luke 11.13

> "If you then, though you are evil, know how to give good gifts to your children, how much more will your Father in heaven give the Holy Spirit to those who ask him!"
> **Luke 11.13**

These words could be paraphrased along the following lines: "There is no conceivable situation in which you could ask for the Holy Spirit and your loving Abba Father would not joyfully give him to you."

Is it really as easy as this? The answer is yes and no! It is as easy as pausing to ask, but so often this gets overlooked. You may find yourself battling on, relying on your own efforts, trying your hardest and often not getting very far at all, when it might be as simple as stopping to ask. The next small catch is to take a moment to receive, to let God speak to you or provide you with whatever you need from him.

God is only a prayer away. This is quite a long way off if you don't actually pray, but a very short distance if you do. As soon as you call upon him, he is with you.

It's all about his presence | 1

‘Jesus said to them, "I tell you the truth, unless you can eat the flesh of the Son of Man and drink his blood, you have no life in you."’

John 6.53

The promise of life, or abundant life as Jesus was later to express it (John 10.10), is something we all long for. It is likely that if a poll was conducted to gauge views about how to obtain this abundant or fullness of life, there would be a variety of opinions that might include material, spiritual and relational ingredients. Jesus put it very bluntly: unless you can eat his flesh and drink his blood, you will never find this life. What does he mean?

Much debate has gone into interpreting these words, but the first thing to note is that direct interaction with Jesus himself is required. It is first and foremost about your relationship with him, and not about material satisfaction or the quality of other human relationships. Perhaps one way of understanding the phrase, 'eating his flesh', is to take his presence seriously.

It is so easy to let other things get in the way of our relationship with God. Once we start to read the Bible as a duty, or prayer becomes an exercise to be fitted into a tight time frame, then perhaps the relationship itself is suffering.

Speak Jesus's name quietly and slowly for a few moments and find something of the truth of his promise that he is there for you now and will always be with you.

It was all for me! | 2

Jesus said to them, "I tell you the truth, unless you can eat the flesh of the Son of Man and drink his blood, you have no life in you."

John 6.53

If eating the flesh of Jesus is to do with engaging with his presence, perhaps drinking his blood is about engaging with his death in a personal way. So what does it mean to engage with Jesus' death?

It is about the love of God. John 3.16 tells us that God loved the world so much that he gave Jesus. Can you accept this invitation to believe he loved you so much that he sent Jesus?

It's about the forgiveness of sins. Can you believe Jesus died for your sins and every sin you have confessed has been totally removed from your record so that God no longer remembers it?

It's about Jesus' total commitment to you. Romans 8.32 says, 'He who did not spare his own Son, but gave him up for us all – how will he not also, along with him, graciously give us all things?' Can you dare to believe this is true for you, and not just a general truth recorded in the Bible? If you are seeking God's healing touch on your life, it can be tempting to think, "Why should God touch me?" The reason is because he has already shown you just how committed he is to you. So why wouldn't he touch you?

Dwell on these truths, worship him for them, and let their power increase in your life.

His gift to us

> 66 *I am going to send you what my Father has promised* 99
> **Luke 24.49**

This is such an inspiring statement to bear in mind as you ponder your dreams and plans for the next few days. Two thousand years ago, Jesus said he was going to send to you what the Father had promised: the Holy Spirit. He has done this and the Spirit of God now hovers over you and your plans like a covering. Nothing can change this. Perhaps the only uncertainty is whether you will pause to remember him, call out to him and draw upon him?

It is like standing under an awning in the rain; the water will not touch you unless you reach up to touch the awning and then the rain will come through. The rain is good; it is the touch of the Holy Spirit upon your activities. He is here and it is up to you to reach up and touch him to allow him to touch you.

See the presence of the Spirit like a blanket stretching over all the events and activities of the next few days, and as you come to each of these moments, call out to him so that he might touch you.

Honest worship

'*Then Solomon began to build the temple of the LORD in Jerusalem on Mount Moriah, where the LORD had appeared to his father David. It was on the threshing-floor of Araunah...*'

2 Chronicles 3.1

This description might seem like a bit too much detail! Wouldn't it have sufficed to say that the temple was built in Jerusalem? However, the details are both fascinating and important.

The threshing-floor of Araunah was a significant place. At the end of 2 Samuel we read that David took a census of his army which, for a number of reasons, displeased God and unleashed his judgment upon David. A plague swept the whole nation, but stopped at the threshing floor of Araunah. It was on this spot that the temple was built.

The significance for us is that worship is not unrelated to reality. When you worship, it is all of you before the Lord, including everything you have been through. You worship him with all that has gone well, as well as with all that has gone badly; you worship him in times of joy and in periods of sadness.

God loves honest worship, worship that springs from who you really are and not just from a voice detached from your heart. Bring all of yourself before God, including those bits you wish were not there.

Extraordinary moments

'Finally, be strong in the Lord and in his mighty power.'

Ephesians 6.10

We all need strength and power. It is all too easy to be aware of our weaknesses, put on a brave face, pretend to be strong, get going and hope for the best! However, Paul is talking about something different here, about us being empowered.

Being 'in the Lord' is really about being in union with Jesus, but surely it could be said that all Christians are automatically in union with him? This is certainly true, but if it was the whole truth then Paul would have no need to write these words. Union with Jesus is both a state in which you live and something into which you can specifically move.

Many people have had experiences of being close to Jesus, and at these times being 'in him' feels very real. However, the challenge is to find the truth of being 'in him' in the ordinary and seemingly humdrum moments of life too.

Next time you are aware of some inner need – strength, patience, love, wisdom, or whatever it is – rather than simply putting on a brave face and ploughing on, pause to remember that you bear God's name and carry his presence within you. In this way, let him change your ordinary moments into something extraordinary.

Be radiant

'When Moses came down from Mount Sinai with the two tablets of the Testimony in his hands, he was not aware that his face was radiant because he had spoken with the LORD.'

Exodus 34.29

Something unique had happened to Moses: he had been with God and his face was shining. God was present with all his people, but because Moses spoke with him 'face to face' (Exodus 33.11) there was something unique about their encounter that had a physical effect upon Moses.

Paul referred to this moment when he talked about the glorious ministry in which we are all a part. In 2 Corinthians 3.7–8 he says that if Moses shone with the glory of God after receiving the law, how much more will we shine with God's glory as we come into contact with the freedom that Christ brings? He goes on to say something even more amazing in verse 18: that our faces all reflect the Lord's glory. We can't see it, but if we could catch a glimpse of the world from the perspective of heaven, we would see the shining faces of those who have turned to Jesus – including your own face shining with his glory.

As you look ahead today, catch the sense that your face is aglow with his presence, glory and peace.

Look out and give thanks

'But when the kindness and love of God our Saviour appeared'

Titus 3.4

The love of God can be such an enormous concept that it can be quite hard to grasp. This verse from Titus puts it in such a beautiful way: it speaks of the kindness of God in Jesus. The word kindness expresses something of Jesus' gentleness and tenderness in his ministry on earth, especially to those who felt undeserving of it, and which he also longs to express to us.

As with so many of the good things God wants to give us, it's important to choose to believe it. Do you really believe God wants to express his goodness to you? If so, watch out for his kindness throughout the day. One way of doing this is to have a short time of review at the beginning or end of each day. Look back and try to detect acts of kindness from the God who loves you, and give thanks for them. It is likely that the more you give thanks, the more you will recognise God's kindness.

Moving on despite fear

Fear is a very powerful force that can stop you in your tracks and render the best of your plans useless. However, this verse contains a few truths.

The first is that fear is not something unique to you. It has plagued individuals in every generation. When fear overwhelms you, what you are experiencing is one of the most common feelings known to human beings.

The second truth in this verse is that fear may be a common experience, but it need not be a complete roadblock. The people in the time of Ezra had a vision. Fear threatened to block them from putting this vision into practice, but they didn't give in and carried on regardless. Their fear was real, but they chose to put it to one side.

Fear itself does not stop you doing anything, but what it does affect is your reaction to it. You certainly don't need to feel guilty about being fearful, but what you are called to do is carry on regardless. It is not courageous to act when you have no fear, but it is when you move ahead despite it.

What are your fears as you face the day ahead? Acknowledge them and walk into the day remembering that you carry the presence of God within you.

Living out what we believe

> *What good is it, my brothers, if a man claims to have faith but has no deeds?*
>
> **James 2.14**

It sounds obvious, but there really should be a link between what we claim to believe and our actions. This is exactly what James was saying in his letter: who we are and the way we act is the test of what we actually believe.

There is a little rhyme that may be familiar: 'If what I believe is true, then what would God have me do?' It is worth keeping this at the forefront of your mind. If you really believe the presence of God is with you in everything you do, what difference should it make to how you approach the things you have to face? If you really believe God has poured his love into your heart, how will this affect the way you are with people? If you really believe Jesus has forgiven your sins, then why do you so easily dwell on your past mistakes?

It is this link between your faith and your actions that is at the heart of Christian character, and it is your character that will be a beacon to those around you.

Take this rhyme and let God use it throughout the day to bind together your faith and your actions. 'If what I believe is true, then what would God have me do?'

He knows!

This verse occurs in the story of the feeding of the 5,000 in John's Gospel. Jesus saw the vast crowd approaching and, although Jesus already knew what he was going to do, he asked Philip where they could possibly buy enough bread for everyone.

There is something remarkably comforting about this. You may not be facing the challenge of having to feed 5,000 hungry people, but you probably face situations where you simply cannot see a way out or do not know what you are meant to do. Find comfort in the knowledge that Jesus sees the situation and knows what to do. Your calling is to catch the fact that Jesus knows, and to learn to trust him. Panic and anxiety will take over if you cannot accept that Jesus knows about the things concerning you, but peace will reign if you believe this.

If there is a situation in your life right now causing you anxiety, take time to ask Jesus for his vision of the situation and let him give you something to lead you towards peace and away from anxiety. What he gives is entirely up to him, and it is not up to you to create the vision, but Jesus longs for you to have peace.

Keeping hold of what God has given you

'*Do not let anyone despise you.*'
Titus 2.15

In many ways this seems like a strange command. If someone chooses to despise you, surely there is nothing you can do about it as you have no control over what other people think? However, Paul is not speaking so much about what people think of you, but more to do with how you react to their opinion of you. Paul wants you to understand that you do not have to let anyone rob you of the wonderful truth of who you are, a precious, loved and cherished child of the Father.

People may think what they will of you for all manner of reasons. Sometimes this is good, at other times it is puzzling. It is so easy to take their thoughts upon yourself and be burdened by the weight of them.

Jesus came so that you can look into his eyes and find the constant, unflinching love of God for you, a love that will never change no matter what you do or have done, and a love so strong that Jesus chose to die for you.

Let no one take that away from you.

> *"Be dressed ready for service and keep your lamps burning ... so that when he comes ..."*
>
> **Luke 12.35**

He is coming – he is here

Passages like this are often thought to apply to a far-off time in the future when the Lord will return, and the assumption is that there is no real impending sense of it happening soon!

However, there is an immediacy about the presence of God that cannot be taken casually. If you were to be told the Lord's return would definitely be tomorrow, of course you would prepare for it in the best way possible, but the challenge is far more than trying to live every day as if this were true. Christians are called to live every moment in the realisation that God is here right now.

The presence of God with you now is even closer than when Jesus walked the earth. When he walked in Galilee, he could not be walking anywhere else, but now his presence with a person in London is as real as his presence with someone in New York, Adelaide, Capetown, or anywhere else in the world.

Jesus, the Lord of all, is with you here, present, watching, active and loving. This is why you should be dressed and ready for service with your lamp kept burning.

The compassion of God

" ...in your great compassion ... "

Nehemiah 9.27

The book of Nehemiah contains part of the account of God's people coming back to him. It is about the rebuilding of the walls in Jerusalem and the people rededicating themselves to God. In chapter 9 they all gather to worship and confess their sins, and in the prayer that is recorded two themes emerge: confession and the compassion of God.

Being convinced of the compassion of God is not simply knowing beyond any shadow of a doubt that God will forgive you no matter what, but it is understanding why he will forgive you. He forgives because of his great compassion. The New Testament goes on to reveal that out of this compassion Jesus died on the cross.

Your sins are not overlooked because God is nice and generous, but because Jesus took the full weight of them on the cross. It was unbearable for God to think that your sins could ever separate you from him, so out of his compassion he gave the equally compassionate Jesus for you.

The compassion of God for you is not just an emotion of his heart, it also led to the death of Jesus on the cross. If you have a cross nearby, hold on to it and find in it the God's compassion for you.

Thank you for your presence

'However, if you suffer as a Christian, do not be ashamed, but praise God that you bear that name.'

1 Peter 4.16

If you had an arrow pointing down to you from heaven marking you out as special, it would be so much easier for you to believe you really are a temple of the Holy Spirit or someone who bears the name of God. However, in today's verse Peter stresses the importance of thanking God for this reality even when the evidence of it cannot be seen, and particularly in moments when you may be experiencing ridicule or suffering because of what you believe.

Awareness of the things of God is often directly in proportion to your ability to give thanks for them. You might be quite good at giving thanks for encouragements, but to give thanks and praise for something you do not yet see demands an element of faith. However, as you begin to give thanks for God's presence, your awareness of it will grow.

This is not just something for your own spiritual satisfaction. As your awareness of God's presence grows, so will your belief that you can make a difference to people around you. You can bring a touch of God's presence, comfort and help to those who need it so much because he really is within you.

Whether or not you sense anything, give thanks for God's promise of his presence. Then walk into the day ahead confident that he is with you.

When things are good...and not so good

Habakkuk really does shine out as a man of faith – not necessarily as a man who lived a life where blessings were showered upon him, but because he could look through the apparent gloom surrounding him and still hold on to the hope that the God who showed himself faithful in the past would prove himself faithful

'Though the fig-tree does not bud and there are no grapes on the vines, though the olive crop fails and the fields produce no food, though there are no sheep in the pen and no cattle in the stalls, yet I will rejoice in the LORD, I will be joyful in God my Saviour.'

Habakkuk 3.17–18

again. His message is beautifully summed up by the sentiment in the verses above: though nothing seems to be going right, I will rejoice in the Lord.

We have come to acquaint blessings with the favour of God, and consequently if things are not going well it's easy to think we are out of favour. This can lead us to a new level of soul-searching as we try to discover what sin may linger within, which sounds very holy except that in fixing our gaze on our souls and sin, we probably have taken our eyes off God. Habakkuk's reaction to apparent failure was to turn his eyes to God and worship him for who he was.

If life is going well, turn your eyes to God and give thanks. If life is not so easy, you still have a calling to turn your eyes to him and worship him anyway. You are not abandoned, nor are you a failure. God is with you.

> '...Andrew, Simon Peter's brother, spoke up, "Here is a boy with five small barley loaves and two small fish, but how far will they go among so many?"'
>
> **John 6.8–9**

What can I possibly do?

In this passage, Andrew asked Jesus a perfectly reasonable question: a hungry crowd was in front of them, Jesus didn't seem to be doing much about it, and the lunch they were looking at was clearly too small! What Andrew did not realise was that he had just presented Jesus with the means of performing a miracle before Andrew's eyes.

Sometimes it is the smallest contribution that becomes the means for a miracle in the hands of Jesus. It might be a brief word of encouragement that changes someone's day, or a small act of kindness that causes someone else to give thanks to God. We simply have no idea what the loaves and fishes we offer can become in Jesus' hands.

It is so tempting to look at your day and wonder what good you can possibly do; perhaps the young boy in the story of the loaves and fishes felt the same. In the hands of Jesus, the smallest thing can touch so many. Have the expectation that you will make a difference today.

God's longing for us

> " *I reared children and brought them up, but they have rebelled against me.* "
> **Isaiah 1.2**

We can catch something of God's deep longing and compassion for us when he shared his heart through Isaiah in this way. There is nothing parents of rebellious children want more than for their children to find the joy of 'home' again.

This is God's heartfelt desire for every one of his children: that they recognise that they are his children and come home. This is not just about everyone else, it is also about you. God's heart is for you to reconnect with him.

Your sense of your relationship with God may be a pattern of 'ups and downs', of times when you sense his closeness and times when you do not. Coming back to him is not about a lifetime of self-discipline, but is summed up in the picture of a young child holding out their arms to their parent. You can do this simply by saying the word 'Abba' or 'Jesus', believing that he is there waiting for you.

It is not that God moves away from you, or how far you wander away from him – he pursues you. It is more likely that you simply turn your eyes away from him and do not notice he is standing there the whole time. He is with you now, so turn to him!

Who is this Jesus? | 1

> In the past God spoke to our forefathers through the prophets at many times and in various ways, but in these last days he has spoken to us by his Son, whom he appointed heir of all things, and through whom he made the universe. The Son is the radiance of God's glory and the exact representation of his being, sustaining all things by his powerful word. After he had provided purification for sins, he sat down at the right hand of the Majesty in heaven.

Hebrews 1.1–3

These verses provide a wonderful seven-fold description of Jesus, so over the next seven days we will look at each phrase.

The first description of Jesus says that God has appointed him as heir of all things. These words can sound formal, but Jesus has already demonstrated the nature of his lordship. For him, it was to take on human form, to live and work on earth and face the humiliation of death at the hands of those over whom he had authority in order that the full power of what he wanted to bring to those in his charge might be released through his death. In other words, Jesus is not an owner surveying his possessions from afar, but someone who has clearly demonstrated his total and utter commitment.

Jesus has demonstrated a sacrificial commitment and passion for you. He longs for you to come afresh to him with confidence, delight in the knowledge of his love and sacrifice and realise how much you mean to him.

It was all made through Jesus | 2

> *...in these last days he has spoken to us by his Son, whom he appointed heir of all things, and through whom he made the universe.*
>
> **Hebrews 1.1–3**

It is through Jesus that the world and everything in it has been made. This means that it is through Jesus that you have been created. Little wonder then that he knows the plans and dreams he has for you, and that he longs to restore you to the person God created you to be.

As a beautifully created person, you have been born into a fallen world which has marred something of this perfection in you, but Jesus came to bring you back to his dream. He could well have shrugged his shoulders and moaned about what human beings have done to his world, but instead he came to restore you. His ministry demonstrated this, as he healed the sick, forgave sinners, challenged injustice and hypocrisy and brought the kingdom and reign of God to a broken world.

As you come to Jesus with your needs, you come to someone who sees the perfection of how you were originally created and who has done whatever it takes for you to be transformed. So you can approach him with wonder, confidence and trust.

> 'The Son is the radiance of God's glory and the exact representation of his being'
>
> **Hebrews 1.1–3**

Jesus and the glory of God | 3

Glory is quite a hard word to define. It is often thought of in terms of light. One way of seeing the glory of God is to see him for who he really is. When Jesus is described as 'the radiance of God's glory' it is because he is the one who reveals what God is really like.

This is important in considering the will of God and what he wants in any given situation. Part of the process of discovering the answer is to look at what Jesus himself did. After all, he is the radiance of God's glory and reveals the wonder of God. What Jesus did was to create an open door into the heart and will of God.

This is very pertinent to the question of sickness and illness. Is it God's desire that you remain sick or could it be he longs for healing for you? In thinking about this a good place to begin is to look at Jesus and determine his attitude to sickness: he healed the sick. Sometimes, as in the case of the man lowered through the roof, Jesus did something else first, whereas at other times, as in the case of Bartimaeus, he responded to the man's immediate need. In his ministry, Jesus revealed God's heart, so let's not settle for anything less.

Representing God | 4

> *The Son is the radiance of God's glory and the exact representation of his being*
>
> **Hebrews 1.1–3**

It was not just the actions of Jesus that reflected what God wanted to do, the very being of Jesus reflected the very being of God. In other words, Jesus' character on earth was exactly as God is. Some people address their prayers to Jesus rather than to the Father or Almighty God, as they see Jesus as somehow more approachable than an austere Father figure. Yet Jesus is crying out, "If you want to know what God is like, look at me."

When Jesus touched those people who were deemed untouchable by others, he reflected the very being of God. In releasing a person from a crowd calling for their death, again, he was reflecting the very nature of God. As Jesus urged forgiveness instead of retribution, once again he reflected exactly what God was and is like.

God the Father, God the Son and God the Holy Spirit are all reflected perfectly in the love which Jesus demonstrated in his ministry. It is wrong to think that one member of the godhead can be approached instead of another. Each person of the Trinity shares the same essential characteristics, and you can approach each with the joy, delight and ease with which you would have approached Jesus in his ministry on earth.

You are deeply loved by the Father, as well as loved by Jesus and the Holy Spirit. You need never be frightened of what they are planning for you. Take a moment to accept the love of the Father, Son and Spirit for you.

> *The Son is the radiance of God's glory and the exact representation of his being, sustaining all things by his powerful word.*
>
> **Hebrews 1.1–3**

Jesus sustains | 5

Many people baulk at the idea of a God who intervenes in their daily life. It seems somehow chaotic to think of God reaching down to do something particular for one person and ignoring the person next to them. However, the reality is that God is already actively involved in your life, sustaining you continually. To ask for God's intervention is not to ask him to suddenly open the door of heaven, miraculously reach down with his hand to do something spectacular and then withdraw to heaven again. Rather, it is up to you to come to God, whose hand is constantly involved in your life. God is already intervening on your behalf to bring all things back to him.

Nor is this sustaining to be regarded as too gentle or something very much in the background. This verse states you are sustained by his powerful word. There is already power at work in your life.

This gives you confidence to believe Jesus is with you all the time and you can find his presence in your life on a daily, even hourly, basis because his powerful, sustaining presence is with you. Prayer begins with you coming to the one who is already present, and calling out for the power which is already at work within you.

Purity | 6

This verse puts the wonder of what Jesus has done for you into such simple language. It is easy to get very burdened about the

> ‘After he had provided purification for sins, he sat down at the right hand of the Majesty in heaven.’
>
> **Hebrews 1.1–3**

extent to which your sins should be confessed and how best to do it, as if the confession itself is what purifies you rather than the self-giving of Jesus. It is first and foremost his action on your behalf that has brought about life-changing forgiveness. In your struggle to find release from sin and to know the reality of forgiveness, you might do better to move beyond the confession itself and turn your heart to praise and worship for all Jesus has done.

This verse also talks about purification for sin, which suggests more than a grudging forgiveness. It is the total release from the stain of your sin upon you; a complete re-clothing in white garments. Again, this is something that has been done for you and is not something you have to make an effort to attain. It is something you can enter into immediately with joy and acceptance.

Jesus is sitting down | 7

'After he had provided purification for sins, he sat down at the right hand of the Majesty in heaven.'

Hebrews 1.1–3

There are three encouraging elements in this statement. First, it implies God's approval for what Jesus had done. All Jesus did, spoke, demonstrated and promised carries with it the echo of God saying, 'Yes.' Some of the promises Jesus made seem almost too good to be true, as if he went a bit too far, but this is not the case. Everything he promised has the stamp of God's approval on it, and is trustworthy because the one who gave the promises is seated in heaven.

This verse also says something about the completeness of Jesus' work; he has completed all he came to do. Whatever needs you might have, Jesus has already come into this world, demonstrated the Father's love, given his life for you and opened the gates of heaven for you. It is not a case of you begging God to reach down and do something, because he has already acted.

Finally, this statement says something wonderful about the approachability of Jesus. A few chapters later, the author of this letter to the Hebrews offers encouragement to come to God's throne with confidence (Hebrews 4.16). Your confidence is based on the fact that the throne you approach is one of grace and mercy because it bears the characteristics of the one who sits on it.

Jesus in all his glory is there for you, reflecting the glory of God. He invites you to come to him and be open to all he has for you.

It's all yours

' "My son," the father said, "you are always with me, and everything I have is yours."

Luke 15.31

The father in the story of the Prodigal Son is so kind to both his sons. To the one who returns from a wayward life there is a welcome back to the family home, and to the resentful older brother an assurance of continuing love. The older brother had seen his life at home in terms of hard work and servitude, and this may have been at the heart of his resentful attitude to his returning younger brother. These beautiful words from the father aimed to change his perspective on his life.

Relationship with God is about his presence with you, not about what you are slavishly meant to do for him. The words in today's verse are a reminder that in Jesus God has given you everything, if you could but open yourself up to receive. The Christian life is about receiving what has been given, not about earning what you think you want.

Take a moment to hear the Father speaking these words to you: "You are always with me, and everything I have is yours." As you let this message touch you, what does it do for you and how will you respond?

Taking hold

Take hold of the eternal life to which you were called...

1 Timothy 6.12

Many people would love life to be different. So many have a conviction that things would be so much better if only life had dealt them a better hand: to live in a nicer part of the world, to have a richer family, more access to education, a chance of employment... the list could go on.

Whoever you are and whatever your circumstances, you have control over some part of your life. You can choose whether to take hold of the life God has for you or let it slip through your fingers. Every single person can take hold of the eternal life to which they were called. Today you can decide to take hold of the forgiveness Jesus offers to you, to choose to believe and stand upon the limitless love of God for you, and to take as true the promise of Jesus to be with you always. No one else can make these decisions for you; it requires a choice from you to take hold of them.

Rather than simply accept what comes along, make these choices now: 'I choose to believe that I am totally forgiven by God, that his love for me is so great it is beyond comprehension and that Jesus is standing right with me now and at all times. I choose to take hold of eternal life.'

Be transformed

...strength and joy in his dwelling-place.

1 Chronicles 16.27

Taking time to find the presence of Jesus with you is a lovely thing to do. However, his presence is not simply a comforting feeling to be enjoyed. It is able to bring something of the transforming power of God to you.

This verse speaks of two specific things that can be found in the presence of God – strength and joy. It is precisely because you may not feel you have either strength or joy that you need this wonderful reminder that they can be found in God's presence. Too often the temptation is to make up for what is lacking by trying to produce it from within yourself, or else pretend you possess what you actually don't have.

As you take a few moments to sit with Jesus, be honest with him about what you need. You do not have to pretend to him to be stronger than you are, or more joyful than may actually be the case. In Mark 10.51, when Jesus asked Bartimaeus what he could do for him, he was inviting him to be utterly honest about his needs. If it is strength (whether physical or mental) or joy you need, be quick to admit your need to Jesus and give him the opportunity to pour his grace upon you.

> **"** *This is what the LORD says... Rescue from the hand of his oppressor the one who has been robbed.* **"**
>
> **Jeremiah 22.3**

Restoring people

When Jeremiah spoke to the king in the name of the Lord, he gave him a message he wanted everyone to hear: rescue those who have been robbed. It is tempting to ask what this has to do with you, but actually you are surrounded by people who have been robbed. Many have had their sense of value, both to God and to others, stolen from them. Psalm 139.15 speaks about how we were all individually created and formed by God. It is this that has been robbed from people. You are surrounded by folk who are discouraged, think their lives are meaningless and lack any real sense of their own worth either to God or to others. How can you be involved in their rescue? One of the answers is by encouragement.

If you can actively spend time each day encouraging someone, it would amount to many people over a fairly short period of time. It might even consist of something as small as speaking to people you would normally ignore or complimenting someone on work well done. Your words might be the only encouragement someone receives, and when you give it you are playing your part in restoring the value that has been robbed from them.

How big are your giants?

Twelve spies were sent out to see if they thought the Israelites could conquer the land of Canaan. Ten of them saw the size of the enemy and warned against such a venture. However, Caleb took a different stance. He fixed his vision on the wonder of God, and not on the size of the enemy. He saw what God could do, and what the Israelites could do because God was with them.

Are you looking forward to the day ahead or are there giants facing you, things that cause a little fear to rise up in you? Remember you are a physical dwelling place of the Holy Spirit. With God living and working in you, everything could change.

Take a few minutes to let the day unfold before you, and recognise the moments that might cause you fear or anxiety. As you look at each situation, remind yourself that you are a temple of the Holy Spirit and you bear the name of the Lord God Almighty. Let God be in those moments and situations before you even get there.

> 'They gave Moses this account: "We went into the land to which you sent us, and it does flow with milk and honey! Here is its fruit. But the people who live there are powerful, and the cities are fortified and very large." ... Then Caleb silenced the people before Moses and said, "We should go up and take possession of the land, for we can certainly do it."'
>
> **Numbers 13.27–28, 30**

Act as if it's true!

> 'Then the cloud covered the Tent of Meeting, and the glory of the LORD filled the tabernacle.'
>
> **Exodus 40.34**

It is not difficult to imagine the hardships, struggles, grumblings and sheer effort of the Israelites wandering in the desert. However, we often overlook the constant presence of God with them. We read that not a day passed without them being fed miraculously, and in addition they would be able to see the presence of God as a cloud by day and as a fire at night, hovering over the tabernacle. Every time an Israelite looked up, they would be able to see this magnificent reminder of the presence of the Lord.

Presumably the constancy of these regular occurrences meant the people began to treat them lightly and regard them as very routine, to the extent that they probably no longer noticed the awesome presence of the Lord with them. Familiarity really did breed contempt.

It is easy to look at the Israelites and judge them, but how lightly do you take the wonder of God within you? You are a living temple of the Holy Spirit, with his very presence dwelling within you as surely as if it were a cloud hovering above your head; in fact even more so, since his presence is not simply with you but in you.

Take hold of this truth: you are a living place where the Spirit of God dwells. Believe it and act as if it were true, because it is!

Start with this

It is good to ... proclaim your love in the morning...

Psalm 92.1–2

Proclaiming God's love for you is one of the most valuable ways of beginning a time of prayer – but why? Does God need reminding that he is loving? Will he be unloving unless you tell him you think he is loving?

Such thoughts paint a strange picture of God! The reason he asks for your worship, or for a proclamation of your love, is not so much for his benefit but because he knows this will be a blessing to you. God is aware that if you start your day by soaking yourself in the wonder of his love for you, your whole attitude to the day will change. You will start the day from a position of resting in his love rather than striving to gain his acceptance.

On a practical level, a helpful way of entering into God's love is to focus on the wonder of 'Abba Father' secure in the knowledge that you have been adopted by him in order that he can share his love with you. Alternatively, think of the wonder of the cross of Christ, not so much to remind yourself of your sins but to focus on the love that drew him to this sacrifice for you.

> **❝** If you seek him, he will be found by you **❞**
>
> **1 Chronicles 28.9**

Searching for God

This beautiful promise is phrased so wonderfully. It does not simply say that if you seek God you will find him, but rather that he will be found by you. One translation puts it this way: "He will let you find him", and another, "He'll make sure you find him." The sense behind it is of God waiting to be found, and guiding your seeking until you do so rather than leaving it up to you to blindly stumble around.

It is tempting to ask, why all the seeking? Why can't God reveal himself to me plainly? Perhaps there is something in the seeking, the waiting and the asking that is precious to him, not in any way gloating, but because it moves him when you spend time actively seeking for him. You might feel the seeking is hard work, frustrating and wears you down, yet it is this searching and hanging on despite everything that is a delight to God.

"He'll make sure you find him." Reflect on moments in the past day when God helped you to find him, and look out for these moments in the day ahead.

A new vision

"Your throne, O God, will last for ever and ever**"**

Hebrews 1.8

The phrase 'for ever and ever' is pretty conclusive! It is a phrase that rules out any ending, so when the writer to the Hebrews spoke of God's throne lasting for ever and ever he was calling us to take seriously the eternal nature of it. However, this is not just about eternity, it is also about the here and now.

This verse also makes it clear that there will never be a situation in which the throne of God is not present, therefore there will never be a situation without hope. Wherever you are, the throne of God is there as well. There is nothing you can do to cause this throne to go away; it will still be there even if you disregard it. What's more, this ever-present throne is not empty. God, whose presence is always with you, sits on the throne.

Take a moment to pause and reflect on the reality of God's throne present with you wherever you may be, and whatever you might be doing throughout the day. You are actually standing before God's throne right now. How does this vision of reality change your perspective?

Acting justly | 1

And what does the LORD require of you? To act justly and to love mercy and to walk humbly with your God.

Micah 6.8

You may spend a lot of time seeking God's will for your life because you don't want to get it wrong. So what does God want of you in any given situation? This verse from Micah reveals something of God's desire for you, which can be applied to most situations and acts as a ready indicator of which way you should turn. It speaks of three attitudes that should rule your life, which we will explore over the next few days.

Standing up for what is right is a means of acting in the cause of justice and truth. You may well have found yourself in an awkward situation where you witness someone being verbally attacked behind their back. A simple word for this is gossip!

There are always two sides to every story, but when gossip is allowed free reign one side of the story gets promoted at the expense of the other. A simple way of acting justly is to walk away from gossip. Yet perhaps your calling is to do more, to be proactive in seeking to present those being talked about in a good light.

In Ephesians 4.29, Paul encouraged believers to speak what was helpful for building people up, and in this they were being imitators of God (Ephesians 5.1). In other words, God is engaged in speaking well of you; his words build you up. When you do this to others you are engaged in a divine activity that is bound to bless you, and will certainly bless others as well.

Loving mercy | 2

God loves it when we are merciful to others, not treating them as they deserve but in a manner that demonstrates forgiveness, blindness to their faults and a willingness always to see the best in them. This invariably means standing back from our immediate reactions to what people have done and making a conscious decision to think and act differently. There can be a cost to this, because deep down we want people to be treated as they deserve. Yet we have to be careful of hypocrisy. Do we want to be treated as we deserve? When we act in a merciful way, it is a reminder of how God treats us. Jesus taking our punishment upon himself on the cross was the very opposite of what we deserve.

There will be many opportunities in the hours ahead to show mercy to others. It may be something small or something much larger – from a kind word to an act of forgiveness. Every time we are merciful, it is a reflection of the unfailing mercy God shows to us.

Walking with God | 3

> *And what does the LORD require of you? To act justly and to love mercy and to walk humbly with your God.*
>
> **Micah 6.8**

Walking humbly with God reveals a different aspect to loving mercy. Yesterday the emphasis was on showing mercy to others, but today the focus is on receiving mercy. Surely we all love to receive mercy, yet we can be strangely reticent about it.

It can be hard to receive God's mercy and forgiveness. Sometimes we may find ourselves wanting to do something to earn it, yet there is nothing we can do. Christ died for our sins, and forgiveness is found in our acceptance of this rather than us working to deserve it. The acceptance of our forgiveness begins when we can stand before the cross, either metaphorically or in front of a real cross, worship Jesus for what he has done for us personally and recognise that we need it.

This can be very hard, but of course the truth is that if we could meet all our own needs we would not need a Saviour. It was because of our helplessness and out of his love that God gave Jesus for us. Stand before him now with honesty and humility.

Serving well

But Martha was distracted by all the preparations that had to be made.

Luke 10.40

Martha gets quite a bad press from the account of her and her sister playing host to Jesus. Mary listened at his feet while Martha prepared everything. So many people who think of themselves as natural 'doers' can feel condemned by Jesus' reaction to her. However, there is no need for self-condemnation, as it was not the fact that Martha was busy that caused Jesus to speak to her. The reason was that she was distracted by everything she was doing.

Serving is a godly activity; it is what Jesus did when he washed the feet of the disciples. In itself, service is a good thing, but not when it becomes a distraction. The time to take stock is when you catch yourself feeling resentful of the service you are doing. At this point you need to pause and find again the relationship with the one who has called you to serve.

One way of keeping distraction and resentment away is to hold fast to the attitude that you are serving Jesus himself, not simply other people. To see Jesus in those whom you serve and to take pleasure in what you are doing in the same way you would if it was for him, really helps you catch his affirming whisper, 'You did it for me.'

Keep looking!

> 'Look to the LORD and his strength; seek his face always.'
> **1 Chronicles 16.11**

When the Bible speaks about the face of God, it is more often than not a reference to his manifest presence. However, this is more than a general presence of God that permeates all creation, it is something we are all urged to be aware of and to seek. This verse also suggests that finding the presence of God should not simply be an encouraging experience, but is important as a means of finding the strength we need for our lives.

This lovely invitation to seek God's face must mean it is possible to do so, as it would be extremely unfair to urge us to do something that is unattainable. In fact, one of the first keys to discovering the presence of God is to recognise that it is meant for you and you can certainly find it. The second key is to realise that the presence of God is not an abstract feeling, but flows from a person: 'Look to the LORD...seek his face.'

As you settle down to pray, and before you say anything to God, take time to assure yourself of his love for you and ask Jesus to be right there. Pay attention to where Jesus is for you and begin to talk to him as you would a friend.

God's vision for you today

May our Lord Jesus Christ himself and God our Father, who loved us and by his grace gave us eternal encouragement and good hope, encourage your hearts and strengthen you in every good deed and word.

2 Thessalonians 2.16–17

This beautiful verse expresses something of God's vision for today. As with many prayers in the Bible, it starts with a reminder of the character of God to whom this appeal is made. God loves his people and has put a real hope into their hearts. If this is true, what comes next can also be relied upon. Paul goes on to express God's vision that his people would be encouraged and strengthened in every good deed and word.

In other words, as you go about your day, setting your hands to do good and helping others when you can, God will be there adding to what you do and blessing this work. Today you carry within you the very presence of God in your heart, and his presence is with you wherever you go and whatever you do.

You may think you have a pretty ordinary life with not much going on, but God thinks differently. Whatever you do, he will be there.

God's pleasure in giving

The actual context for this verse is the thorny subject of money. Jesus had been urging his disciples not to worry about such things as food and drink, because God could supply all of these in abundance. Jesus went on to sum up God's attitude to his people with these words, "... your Father has been pleased to give you the kingdom."

The first thing to note is that this verse speaks about God's pleasure. Any sense you may have of the grudging nature of God's love for you should dissolve in the light of this verse, which encourages a lovely image of Abba Father delighting in his children and looking at them with pleasure. This is the truth – God delights in you.

The verse goes on to say that it is God's kingdom which he is pleased to give you. Since Jesus is the king, the kingdom flows as a natural extension of his reign and rule. In other words, the Father's delight is to release the kingdom wherever it is invited, so the things Jesus came to bring can be released when the door is opened.

As you look at the need in your own life or in the lives of those for whom you pray, a good question to consider is what aspect of the kingdom the Father wants to bring to each particular need or situation. Then pray for it – not to a God who is grudging in his gifts but to the one who delights to give his kingdom to you.

God's delight

'...he rescued
me because he
delighted in me.'

Psalm 18.19

Why would God want to do something for you? You may look at your past and wonder what God sees in it, and look at the future and despair that anything will come of it. This verse cuts straight through this type of self-analysis; God acts because he delights in you.

This in itself raises all manner of questions. Why would God delight in you? What have you ever done that would make the Lord God, who created heaven and earth, delight in you? He tolerates you, maybe, but does he really delight in you?

The rest of Psalm 18 implies that God's delight in David was because he was good and faithful in all he did. Yet in Psalm 51, the psalm David composed after committing his sin with Bathsheba, his confidence in the love of God is still shining through and he speaks of coming to God still trusting in his 'unfailing love'.

God's delight in you is not based on your actions or achievements, but simply on his unfailing and unalterable love for you.

When the Queen of Sheba heard about the fame of Solomon and his relation to the name of the LORD, she came to test him with hard questions.

1 Kings 10.1

Having a relationship with his name

In some ways this is quite a strange phrase! Normally a relationship is with a person, but here it appears to be with a name. The phrase is probably alluding to King Solomon's intimacy with God. The Bible speaks of Solomon's wisdom, but this phrase reveals that his wisdom was not a gift dropped from on high, but rather that it flowed out of his intimate relationship with God.

Intimacy with God is probably also your aim. Jesus came in order that you might have a relationship with his name, or his presence, so that the love the Father had for him might also be within you (John 17.26). A natural consequence of this intimacy is that the things of God will naturally flow through you. What you have will be so attractive to others that they will want to know the source of it, which is your intimacy with Jesus – a relationship with his name.

Return to these wonderful words in Jeremiah 15.16 and focus on them for a few minutes: '…I bear your name, O LORD God Almighty.' His presence is here, his intimacy is here and whatever you need from him is also here.

When in need, look up

The story of the bronze serpent is a powerful story. The Israelites moaned to God, who responded with judgment that came in the form of a plague of poisonous snakes. After crying out for mercy, Moses was instructed by God to make a bronze serpent so that anyone who looked at it would be healed.

> 'The LORD said to Moses, "Make a snake and put it up on a pole; anyone who is bitten can look at it and live." So Moses made a bronze snake and put it up on a pole. Then when anyone was bitten by a snake and looked at the bronze snake, he lived.'
>
> **Numbers 21.8–9**

Jesus used this story to talk about himself, saying that he would be lifted up in the same way as the bronze serpent (John 3.14).

The people called out for God to take away the snakes. Instead he provided a means of healing when the people were bitten. We want God to take away the evil and pain in our lives. Sometimes he may do this and sometimes he may not, but what he has done is to provide a means of healing when hardships come.

The means of healing in the above story was the provision of the bronze snake, so that when pain really set in the people could turn their attention away from this by looking at the bronze sign of healing. Taking your immediate gaze off your suffering and turning it on to Jesus should always be the first step to take when things go wrong. He is there so look to him.

The unseen hand of God

So Pharaoh sent for Joseph, and he was quickly brought from the dungeon.

Genesis 41.14

The story of Joseph – the depths to which he sank and the heights he rose to – is an amazing story of human adventure and divine planning. It says there is always hope because God really can use everything to suit his purposes. He used the arrogance of a young man and the jealousy of his brothers to bring about an extraordinary act of deliverance for a whole nation. This story reveals the unseen hand of God constantly at work to bring about his purposes.

There is no record of what was going on in Joseph's heart during his years of hardship and imprisonment, but it is apparent that the man who emerged from these difficult times was a man free from anger and with no desire to punish others. In short, a man who could see the hand of God in all that had happened to him.

It is so easy to worry about whether God can ever use you. Have you done something to rule yourself out of his plan? Did you miss the course he had marked out for you? The calling is to trust him and, like Joseph, to hold firm to the belief that God is at work in all that may happen to you.

Take a moment at the end of this day to reflect on God's hand at work whether or not you could see it or were aware of it. Give God thanks that nothing in this day has been wasted because he has been there.

How do we worship?

'David and the whole house of Israel were celebrating with all their might before the LORD, with songs and with harps, lyres, tambourines, sistrums and cymbals.'

2 Samuel 6.5

Worship is meant to be one of the most wonderful things in the world, something that reflects the wonder of what is going on in heaven. Yet all too often our experience of worship doesn't seem to reflect this. One of the reasons is to do with what we put into it.

When we read of David and his men celebrating with 'all their might', the picture is one of them putting their energy into what they were doing, and not letting other people do it for them.

This isn't an invitation to take castanets and drums with you to your next church service, but rather to recognise that what you get out of worship is very much linked to what you put in to it. You can sing a hymn or song as a passive action, or you can give the words your attention and let your heart be touched by what you are singing. This is a choice that you, and only you, can make.

The next time you are in church, or even worshipping on your own right now, reflect on how much you are putting into it or whether is it simply happening around you with little involvement on your part.

The throne of Grace | 1

> 'Let us then approach the throne of grace with confidence, so that we may receive mercy and find grace to help us in our time of need.'
>
> **Hebrews 4.16**

Over the next few days, some of the different elements in this lovely invitation will be explored. Today the focus is on what is standing at the centre of this verse: a throne of grace.

No matter how benevolent is the monarch who sits on this throne, the two words 'throne' and 'grace' are not normally associated with each other. There is etiquette about approaching kings and queens. Not everyone is allowed near, and it has to be done in a particular way following certain rules. The concept of a throne of grace is different. Not only is it a throne associated with love and kindness, it is associated with what God has already done. He has already opened the door for you to come in, given you the invitation and prepared for your arrival.

As you ponder approaching God for any reason, the answer is an immediate 'come'. You may not be able to guarantee the exact answer you will receive, but you can guarantee your reception. Whatever is on your heart, God bids you come.

Living in the presence of the throne of God | 2

> *Let us then approach the throne of grace with confidence, so that we may receive mercy and find grace to help us in our time of need.*
>
> **Hebrews 4.16**

The accessibility of God's throne comes with a challenge: you are invited to approach it. In other words, the throne exists all the time, but are you present before it? The open invitation to approach means you have to respond; you can choose to act on it or not. How?

The throne of grace can be thought of as an image of Jesus, representing his powerful yet kind presence. Quietly speaking his name begins the approach to his throne. As you do this, you recall his presence and also step into it.

Ponder your plans for the hours ahead of you, and as they go through your mind speak the name of Jesus over them. As you focus on his presence before these events take place, it is likely you will recall his presence with you as you face them in reality.

Whether or not you remember Jesus, every part of your day will take place before his throne. What will make a difference to you is your awareness of it.

Coming to God with confidence | 3

> *Let us then approach the throne of grace with confidence, so that we may receive mercy and find grace to help us in our time of need.*
>
> **Hebrews 4.16**

Sometimes it is not so much a matter of what you do, but how you do it. Prayer is one of these things. This verse gives a clear indication of the 'right way' to pray and it is not about the words to use or the pattern to follow, but rather it is about the attitude of your heart. You are encouraged to have confidence in your prayers. Another possible translation of the word would be 'boldness'.

All too often it is easy to be somewhat sheepish in prayer, perhaps because you are aware of your failings and smallness compared to God's greatness. This sounds like a good and honest response to God, but it isn't biblical. You are called to pray with confidence and boldness.

Your confidence is based on a number of truths: no matter what you have done, you come into the presence of the one who utterly loves you. Not only does he love you, but he is thrilled and delighted to see you. It matters to him that you are in his presence, and he misses you when you are not there.

Choose to believe in his pleasure in you and come before him now.

The mercy and grace of God | 4

> *Let us then approach the throne of grace with confidence, so that we may receive mercy and find grace to help us in our time of need.*
>
> **Hebrews 4.16**

Mercy and grace are all about receiving the kindness you do not deserve. It can be very easy to attempt to justify yourself before God and ask him to answer your prayers because of what you have done. However, this verse puts God's help to you in an altogether different category. The help God gives is not a reward, it is mercy and grace. It is about him, not you.

This message is shown by Jesus' action on the cross. He gave his life for you as an act of mercy and not because you asked him to do so. The activity of God involving you is his initiative.

So when you come to God in prayer with needs you want to bring to him, begin by looking at the cross rather than being concerned with how good or bad you have been. His answer to your prayers will be acts of mercy and grace.

If you have a particular need for which you are praying, begin by holding an image of the cross before you. The mercy demonstrated by this action is the same mercy that flows out of his heart for all that you need.

> 'Let us then approach the throne of grace with confidence, so that we may receive mercy and find grace to help us in our time of need.'

Hebrews 4.16

Seeing God at work | 5

The final revelation in this verse is that the help God gives is real help; it is relevant to your need. It is not just general kindness that is required when you are in need, but something specific to the particular need, and this is exactly what this verse says you will receive. This is not the same as saying God will give you everything you ask for, but it is an invitation to bring every need to him in confident expectation.

It is wonderful to confidently hand your concerns over to God, but what is easily overlooked is the process of looking back to work out where God's help was and what he provided. It is often only at this point that the hand of God can be seen and appreciated.

As you ponder the past 24 hours, call your prayers to mind and think about what happened in these situations. Reflect on the help God gave and where his hand was at work. Give thanks and walk into the day ahead with greater confidence.

Worship is saying to God, "You are right!"

"Well said, teacher," the man replied. *"You are right..."*

Mark 12.32

These words, spoken by an unnamed teacher of the law in Mark's Gospel, contain the heart of worship. It is about taking the words of Jesus and being able to say, "You are right."

Of course, we know Jesus is right – that is why we follow him – but it is amazing how many of our inner thoughts are at odds with the heart of Jesus, such as when we doubt the love of God, feel anxious that he will not look after us, withhold forgiveness from another person or doubt the forgiveness of God for us. These are all matters about which Jesus has spoken and revealed the Father's heart. To each of these, our response should be to say to Jesus, "You are right."

The reason this matters is because Jesus taught these things so that by hearing them and submitting to them, we might begin to find the fullness of life that he came to give us.

Is there one of these areas or issues that causes you a particular struggle? Take some time to discover what Jesus says about this particular area. What are the words from the Gospels that are relevant to your situation? Listen to him, and begin to say to him, "You are right."

> "*Peace I leave with you; my peace I give you. I do not give to you as the world gives. Do not let your hearts be troubled and do not be afraid.*"

John 14.27

The beginning of peace

Peace is a word often mentioned over this Christmas season. It is a word that sits well with images of snow-covered fields, families enjoying each other's company and people laying aside their own needs for the happiness of others. It is all very well if this is the reality of Christmas for you, but if not, are you destined to miss out on experiencing this elusive thing known as 'peace'?

The startling message of Jesus in this passage is that whatever worldly images seem to convey peace, they are actually nothing like the peace he promises which flows from his presence. Jesus is not present to judge or criticise, but to be there for you in times of hurt, brokenness, disappointment, weariness and tiredness.

Finding Jesus' peace starts with you acknowledging this wonderful truth: he is with you right now, despite whatever else may be going on in your life. This is the truth, but you need to acknowledge it and tune into it. Wherever you might be right now, pause to reflect on his presence with you and share with him whatever is on your heart. This is the beginning of peace.

Exploring Christmas

> *"I have come into the world as a light, so that no one who believes in me should stay in darkness."*
>
> **John 12.46**

This verse is a challenge to take Christmas even more seriously. Have you fully appreciated why Jesus came for you? Jesus said he came as light, so no one who has accepted him should remain in darkness. He is speaking about all of us, including you; he does not want you, or any part of you, to remain in darkness.

You can probably accept this, but deep down, if you are honest, there are bits of you that remain hidden away, parts that exercise a less-than-helpful influence upon the rest of your life. Jesus came to bring change.

The first step to finding change is not to feel guilty. Very often it is guilt that causes things to get hidden away in the first place, even seeking to hide them away from Jesus. Words like 'confession' and 'repentance' can sound very threatening, but at the heart of them is simply the admission that this is what it is like for you, even though you may wish it were not so.

The next step is equally gentle: ask Jesus to touch these dark places with his light and with all the love that drew you to him in the first place. Wait and see what he does.

Come, Lord Jesus, come.

The risk God takes with us

> '...an angel of the Lord appeared to him in a dream and said, "Joseph son of David, do not be afraid to take Mary home as your wife, because what is conceived in her is from the Holy Spirit."'

Matthew 1.20

The Christmas story contains a lot of risk! At any point one of the main characters could have decided they'd had enough and wanted out! Another possibility is they could have decided to do things a different way if they were not happy with the choices God seemed to have made. Yet throughout, people were committed to following God's plan.

God actually takes a risk with all of us. He trusts us with his love, his presence and with being his ambassadors to the people we will come across each day. For some of the people you will meet, you will be the only one of God's ambassadors they will come across. God trusts you with this.

You may be someone's only contact with God today, so why not make a determined effort to ensure every contact counts? It doesn't necessarily mean you have to step out of your comfort zone, but simply bear it in mind that you represent God and carry his presence. Then your speaking, listening and actions, however small, will take on a whole new perspective.

The perfect relationship

> **"**...miserable comforters are you all!**"**
>
> **Job 16.2**

Sadly, it is so easy to judge people for what they are going through, to look at their hardships, think you can see the reasons for their suffering and judge them.

Job was on the receiving end of this. Untold misery had come upon him and his friends thought they knew exactly why he was suffering, so they let him have the benefit of their wisdom! This certainly did not bless Job so he called them 'miserable comforters!'

Christmas is approaching and there can be no greater contrast to Job's miserable comforters than Jesus. Jesus is uniquely positioned to see your life and give you a very honest lecture about why you go through what you do – but he never does this. He saw the plight of humanity, and despite everything it would cost him he came to this earth to communicate the love of God and the way to peace in this troubled world.

You may be in difficulty of some kind, or life might be very challenging for you over this particular season. Jesus wants to be here with you, not to lecture you or make you feel guilty, but to lift you out of the pit and give you peace in your heart. Whatever life holds for you at the moment, share your situation with the one who came to transform you.

Being like Jesus

> '...if we love one another, God lives in us and his love is made complete in us.'
>
> **1 John 4.12**

The message of the Saviour who has come to you personally is not meant to make you like a reservoir, storing up the blessings of God within you. His message is meant to make you like an irrigation channel with water flowing in and through you. You are then in a position to give out something of what you have received from God, rather than what is unnatural or foreign to you.

As you prepare for Christmas, including fellowship with others, a wonderful but challenging place to start is to look at 1 Corinthians 13. This chapter about love can be seen as a description of the nature of the love of God, as well as a description of how you are to be with others. This love is what the world needs, it is what the people you will meet over Christmas need, what you yourself need and what has been given to you by God in Jesus.

As a guideline for enjoying fellowship with others over this season and beyond, behave as Jesus would with the people you meet.

Gifts in abundance

Happy Christmas!

'Mercy, peace and love be yours in abundance.'

Jude 2

The way Jude begins his letter is probably a standard greeting, but actually these words sum up what Christmas is about. Christmas is the mercy, peace and love of God towards you in abundance.

Just a touch of God's love would be wonderful and life-transforming, just a small dose of God's mercy is probably all that's deserved and just a few moments of peace would be a welcome break. Yet when Jesus came to this world, when he came to you, it was far more than a touch of God's love, mercy and peace. It was the entire love, mercy and peace of God in human form. This is God's gift to the world; this is God's gift to you.

As you mull over something of the truth of Christmas today, among all the other things that go to make this a special day, ponder something of the abundance of God towards you. In Jesus he gave you all the mercy, peace and love of God you could ever need.

Reflect on it, be open to it and worship him for it.

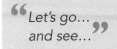

Luke 2.15

" *Let's go...* *and see...* **"**

Christ has come

Christmas Day may have come and gone, the preparations may or may not have been worth all the effort, the big day is over, but the truth remains – Christ Jesus has come. These days following Christmas are opportunities to echo the feelings of the shepherds: "Let's go to Bethlehem and see this thing that has happened, which the Lord has told us about." Let's take some time to explore this great truth: Jesus Christ, God in human form, has come into this world.

It is not simply that Jesus has come into the world, but that he is here for you. What difference does it make knowing that at every single moment there is someone with you who loves you so much he came to be part of your life? It takes a few moments to take all this in.

Perhaps the chaos of Christmas surrounds you? Maybe you are joyful, or possibly sad? However you feel, this statement is true: Christ is with you. Why not take a few moments to make these words personal: "Jesus Christ is with me right now, in my life and in my situation. He has come to share my life with me and to let me share in all he has for me."

Being changed by prayer

Little reason is given about why people should enter through one gate and leave by another! Perhaps it was something to do with keeping the crowds under control? However, this slightly strange passage about where you come in and go out actually contains a valuable message. The experience of coming into the presence of the Lord should change you; you should come out from it different to how you went in to it.

> "When the people of the land come before the LORD at the appointed feasts, whoever enters by the north gate to worship is to go out by the south gate; and whoever enters by the south gate is to go out by the north gate. No-one is to return through the gate by which he entered, but each is to go out by the opposite gate."
>
> **Ezekiel 46.9**

Certainly, this season of Christmas should bring change as we celebrate the wonder of Jesus coming to live among us. Yet this message is about more than Christmas: it is about every encounter you have with God. God's desire is that you take seriously what he communicates to you. It might be a verse as you read the Bible, a picture which comes to mind or a feeling of peace as you pray about something. It is important not to let such things slip away, but hold on to them and perhaps write them down so they last longer than your immediate memory. Then pause and let whatever God says have an impact upon you: why you need to be told this and why is he saying this to you today.

Our salvation

> *"For my eyes have seen your salvation"*
>
> **Luke 2.30**

There is a beautiful moment just before this verse when Simeon sees the baby Jesus. He had been told by God that he would one day see the promised Messiah, so what was he expecting to see? What were his expectations of a Messiah? Perhaps he was looking out for power and glory, or an end to the oppressive government? The reality is, he saw a baby! This little one was the promised salvation of God, a vulnerable newborn so easy to ignore and seemingly so powerless.

This is your salvation too. The one who entered this world and experienced what it was like to grow up and struggle with the hardships of being a refugee is your salvation. Far from being powerless, it is this vulnerability that gives Jesus the power and authority to be the Saviour.

As you approach God today, he knows and understands your life. He actually shares the reality of humanity and chose to experience it so that his call for you to trust him would not be an idle call, but rather a voice of love.

Being a part of his story

"Do you understand what I have done for you?"

John 13.12

Jesus asked his disciples this question after he had washed their feet. He asked them to reflect on what he had done and apply the lesson to their lives. He might well ask you the same question in these days after Christmas. Do you really understand what he has done for you? It is all too easy to get caught up in the 'sweetness' of the story – mangers, angels, shepherds and stars – and lose the raw impact of God himself coming for his people, for you.

When Jesus washed the feet of his disciples, it was not an occasion for his followers to simply observe, it was a deeply personal act for each of them. However, unless they chose to apply it personally they were going to miss out on so much, including a relationship with him.

"Do you understand what I have done for you?" This is your challenge over Christmas. Find again the relevance of Jesus coming for you. Make it personal, and discover the joy of being part of his story.

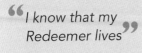

I know that my Redeemer lives

Job 19.25

He is here for me

Despite all Job was going through, all he had lost and all the well-meaning clichés fed to him, Job looked up to his God and said these amazing words, "I know that my Redeemer lives."

You may be in a hard place at this time, perhaps calling out to God for healing or facing discouragement in some way. The wonder of this season of Christmas is that Jesus has come for you. He is your Redeemer, Saviour and hope. Let every picture of the nativity you see on the Christmas cards around you, every mention of the word 'Jesus' you hear in the carols being sung or even piped through the shops, can be a reminder to you that Jesus has come. Then let this truth cause you to proclaim with Job that despite everything else going on in your life, your health or your circumstances, 'I know that my Redeemer lives.'

Repeat this phrase a few times, and as you do so concentrate on a different word within it. Know that Jesus lives and capture the certainty of it. Focus on 'my Redeemer' and recognise that he came for you. Call him 'Redeemer', as he came to lift your life out of the pit, and because he stands with you, alive and active. Know that Jesus really lives.

Not a judge but a saviour

For I did not come to judge the world, but to save it.

John 12.47

As you prepare to embrace another new year, this is a natural day to reflect on the past 12 months. What comes naturally to mind? It may be happy events and pleasing achievements, or mistakes made and disappointments that have shaken you. Spend a little time bringing the past year to Jesus with your joys, sadnesses and disappointments.

It is right and natural to rejoice in the blessings of God and let them turn to praise as you remember happy times. However, if you are struggling with disappointment about something, turn to the truth of Lamentations 3.22–23 and remember that tomorrow is a new day: '…his compassions never fail. They are new every morning.' It may be that you long for comfort as you feel bowed low by regret, in which case call to mind these words of Jesus that he did not come to judge, but to save. His presence with you transforms you from one who is crushed to one who bears fruit.

Jesus came as our Saviour, not as our judge. He is not seeking to condemn anyone or anything in this past year, but he does want to bring you hope and change in the days to come.

Index